Copyright, © 2018 by Patti Hanni, Denison, Texas.

All rights reserved. No part of this book may be reproduced in any form or by any means without permission from Patti Hanni.

ISBN-13 978-0-9843326-5-6

Library of Congress Control Number: 2018949246

Published by:

Pearson Jagoe Publishing
600 Ambassador Street
Denison, Texas 75020

ACKNOWLEDGEMENT

Thank you
Woodsong Institute of Art
Marylyn Todd Daniels
Laura Strong
For inspiring me

CREDITS

Unless otherwise noted, all scripture references and quotations are from the New King James study Version of the Bible. Copyright 1997, 2007 by Thomas Nelson, Inc.

Front cover photograph by Emily Roth
All other Photographs by Patti Hanni
Cover production: Robert Wayne Massey
Base Maps courtesy of Woodsong Institute of Art
Details on all maps by Patti Hanni

TABLE OF CONTENTS

BOOK	PAGE
Ecclesiastes	1
Hosea	37
Joel	79
Obadiah	95
Jonah	105
Nahum	123
Haggai	137

A Book Study of Ecclesiastes

ECCLESIASTES

INTRODUCTION

The Book of Ecclesiastes is one of the most misunderstood books in the Bible. Christians have tended either to ignore the message of the book or regard it as testimony of a man living apart from God. This is unfortunate, for the book asks relevant, searching questions about the meaning of life, and it declares utter futility of an existence without God. Like all scripture, the book of Ecclesiastes benefits and edifies God's people. I pray you read along and dig into scripture to grasp the morsel that are tucked within the scriptures.

The author, Solomon referred to himself as the Teacher, or leader of the assembly. He was both assembling people to hear a message and gathering wise sayings. Solomon, one person in the Bible who had everything, wisdom, power, riches honor reputation, God's favor, is the one who discussed the ultimate emptiness of all that this world has to offer. He tried to destroy people's confidence in their own efforts, abilities, and righteousness and direct them to commitment to God as the only reason for living.

CHAPTER 1:1-18

Solomon had a purpose for writing skeptically and pessimistically. Near the end of his life, he looked back over everything he had done, and most of it seemed meaningless. A common belief was that only good people prospered and that only the wicked suffered, but that had not proven true in his experience. Solomon wrote this book after he had tried everything and achieved much, only to find that nothing apart from God made him happy. He wanted his readers to avoid these same senseless pursuits. If we try to find meaning in our accomplishments rather than in God, we will never be satisfied and everything we pursue will become meaningless. Solomon's kingdom, Israel was in its golden age, but Solomon wanted the people to understand that success and prosperity do not last long, (Psalm 103:14-16; Isaiah 40:6-8; James 4:14). All human accomplishments will one day disappear, and we must keep this in mind to live wisely. If we do not, we will become either proud and self-sufficient when we succeed or sorely disappointed when we fail. Solomon's goal was to show that earthly possessions and accomplishments are ultimately meaningless. Only the pursuit of God brings real satisfaction. We should honor God in all we say, think, and do.

Many people feel restless and dissatisfied. They wonder: (1) If I am in God's will, why am I so tired and unfulfilled? (2) What is the meaning of life? (3) When I look back on it all will I be happy with my accomplishments? (4) Why do I feel burned out, disillusioned, dry? (5) What is to become of me? Solomon tests our faith, challenging us to find true and lasting meaning in God alone. As you take a hard look at your life, as Solomon did his, you will see how important serving God is over all other options. Perhaps God is asking you to rethink your purpose and direction in life, just as Solomon did in Ecclesiastes.

"What is wrong cannot be righted. What is missing cannot be recovered" refers to the ultimate perplexity and confusion that come to us because of all the unanswered questions in life. Solomon, writing about his own life, discovered that neither his accomplishments nor his wisdom could make him truly happy. True wisdom is found in God and true happiness comes from pleasing him.

The more you understand, the greater your pain and difficulty. For example, the more you know, the more imperfection you see around you; and the more you observe, the more evil becomes evident. As you set out with Solomon to find the meaning of life, you must be ready to feel more, think more, question more, hurt more, and do more. Are you ready to pay the price for wisdom? Solomon highlights two kinds of wisdom in the book of Ecclesiastes: (1) human knowledge, reasoning, or philosophy, and (2) the wisdom that comes from God. In verses 16-18, Solomon is talking about human knowledge. When human knowledge ignores God, it only highlights our problems because it cannot provide the answers without God's eternal perspective and solution.

CHAPTER 2:1-26

Solomon conducted a search for life's meaning as an experiment. He first tried pursuing pleasure. He undertook great projects, bought slaves and herds and flocks, amassed wealth, acquired singers, added many concubines to his harem, and became the greatest person in Jerusalem. But none of these gave him satisfaction. But as he looked at everything he had worked so hard to accomplish, it was all so meaningless. It was like chasing the wind. There is really nothing worthwhile anywhere. Some pleasures Solomon sought were wrong and some were worthy, but even the worthy pursuits were futile when he pursued them as an end in themselves. We must look beyond our activities to the reasons we do them and the purpose they fulfill. Is your goal in life to search for meaning or to pursue God, who gives meaning?

Solomon built houses, a temple, a kingdom, a family (1 Kings 3-11). In the course of history, they would all be ruined. In Psalm 127:1, Solomon wrote, "Unless the LORD builds a house, the work of the builders is useless. Unless the LORD protects a city, guarding it with sentries will do no good." This book is part of Solomon's testimony as to what happens to a kingdom or family that forgets God. As you examine your projects or goals, what is your starting point, your motivation? Without God as your foundation, all you are living for is meaningless. Solomon summarized his many attempts at finding life's meaning as "chasing the wind." We feel the wind as it passes, but we cannot catch hold of it or keep it. In all our accomplishments, even the big ones, our good feelings are only temporary. Security and self-worth are not found in these accomplishments, but far beyond them in the love of God. Think about what you consider worthwhile in your life—where you place your time, energy, and money. Will you one day look back and decide that these too were a "chasing the wind?" Solomon realized that wisdom alone cannot guarantee eternal life. Wisdom, riches, and personal achievement matter very little after death—and everyone must die. We must not build our life on perishable pursuits, but on the solid foundation of God. Then even if everything we have is taken away, we still will have God, who is all we really need anyway. Is death the ultimate equalizer of all people, no matter what they attained in life? While this appears to be true from an earthly perspective, God makes it clear that what we do here has a great impact upon our eternal reward. Solomon continues to show that hard work bears no lasting fruit for those who work solely to earn money and gain possessions. Not only will everything be left behind at death, but it may be left to those who have done nothing to earn it. Hard work done with proper motives is not wrong. We must work to survive, and, more important, we are responsible for the physical and spiritual well-being of those under our care. But the fruit of hard work done to glorify only ourselves will be passed on to those who may later lose or spoil it all. Such toil often leads to grief, while serving God leads to everlasting joy.

Why are you working so hard? Is Solomon recommending we make life a big irresponsible party? No, he is encouraging us to take pleasure in what we are doing now and to enjoy life because it comes from God's hand. True enjoyment in life comes only as we follow God's guidelines for living. Without him, satisfaction is a lost search. Those who really know how to enjoy life are the ones who take life each day as a gift from God. Thanking him for it and serving him in it. Those without God will have no relief from toil and no direction to guide them through life's complications.

Ecclesiastes

CHAPTER 3:1-22

Verses 1-8 were a song sung by the Byrd's in late 1965.

Solomon's point here is that God has a plan for all people. Thus, he provides cycles of life, each with its work for us to do. Although we may face many problems that seem to contradict God's plan, these should not be barriers to believing in him, but rather opportunities to discover that without God, life's problems have no lasting solutions!

Timing is important. All experiences listed in these verses are appropriate at certain times. The secret to peace with God is to discover, accept, and appreciate God's perfect timing. The danger is to doubt or resent God's timing. This can lead to despair, rebellion, or moving ahead without his advice. When is there time for hating? We should not hate evil people, but we should hate what they do. We should also hate it when people are mistreated, when children are starving and when God is being dishonored. In addition, we must hate the sin in our life—this is God's attitude (Psalm 5:5). Your ability to find satisfaction in your work depends on your attitude. You will become dissatisfied if you lose the sense of purpose God intended for your work. We can enjoy our work if we remember that God has given us work to do and, realize that the fruit of our labor is a gift from him. See your work as a way to serve God. God has planted eternity in the human heart. This means that we can never be completely satisfied with earthly pleasures and pursuits. Because we are created in God's image, we have a spiritual thirst, we have eternal value, and nothing but the eternal God can truly satisfy us. He has built in us a restless yearning for the kind of perfect world that can only be found in his perfect rule. He has given us a glimpse of the perfection of his creation. But it is only a glimpse; we cannot see into the future or comprehend everything. So, we must trust him now and do his work on earth.

To be happy and do good are worthy goals for life, but we can pursue them in the wrong way. God wants us to enjoy life. When we have the proper view of God, real pleasure is found in enjoying our gifts from God, not in what we accumulate. What is the purpose of life? It is that we should fear the all-powerful God. To fear God means to respect and stand in awe of him because of who he is. Purpose in life starts with whom we know; not what we know or how good we are. It is impossible to fulfill our God-given purpose unless you revere God and give him first place in your life.

Solomon reflects on several apparent contradictions in God's control of the world. There is evil and corruption in the place where there should be justice. It even affects the legal system. Solomon asked how God's plan can be perfect when there is so much injustice and oppression in the world. God does not ignore injustice but will bring it to an end at his appointed time. It is easy to use such contradictions as excuses to not believe in God, but Solomon used them to show how we can honestly look at life's problems and still keep our faith. This life is not all there is, yet even in this life we should not pass judgment on God because we do not know everything. God's plan is for us to live forever with him. So, live with eternal values in view, realizing that all contradictions will one day be cleared up by the Creator himself.

Our bodies cannot live forever in their present state. In that sense, humans and animals are alike. But Solomon acknowledged that God has given people the hope of eternity and that we will undergo judgment in the next life—making us different from animals. Because we have eternity planted in our heart, we have a unique purpose in God's overall plan. Yet, we cannot discover God's purpose for our life by our own efforts—only through building a relationship with God and seeking his guidance. Are you now living as God wants? Do you see life as a gift from him?

CHAPTER 4:1-16

Some people are lazy while others are workaholics. The lazy person, seeing the futility of dashing about for success, idles his time away and hurts both himself and those who depend on him. The workaholics are often driven by greed, envy, and a distant desire to stay ahead of everyone else. Both extremes are foolish and irresponsible. The answer is to work hard, but with moderation. Take time to enjoy the gifts God has given, and realize it is God who gives the assignments and the rewards, not us.

There are advantages to cooperating with others. Life is designed for companionship, not isolation, for intimacy, not loneliness. Some people prefer isolation, thinking they cannot trust anyone. We are not here on earth to serve ourselves, but to serve God and others. Do not isolate by yourself and try to go it alone. Seek companions, be a team member.

Advancement or getting to the top is meaningless. Position, popularity, and prestige are poor goals for a life's work. Although many seek these, they are shadows without substance. Many people seek recognition for their accomplishments, but people are fickle, changing quickly and easily. How much better to seek God's approval. His love never changes.

CHAPTER 5:1-20

When we enter the house of God, we should have the attitude of being open and ready to listen to God, not to dictate to Him what we think he should do.

Solomon warns us about making foolish promises to God. In Israelite culture, making vows was a serious matter. Vows were voluntary, but once made they were unbreakable (Deuteronomy 23:21-23). It is foolish to make a promise you cannot keep or to play games with God by only partially fulfilling your vow (Proverbs 20:25). It is better not to make a vow than to make a vow to God and break it. If you make a vow, keep it.

We always want more than we have. Solomon observed that those who spend their lives obsessively seeking after money never find the happiness it promises. Wealth attracts freeloaders and thieves, causes sleeplessness and fear, and ultimately ends in loss because it must be left behind (Mark 10:23-25; Luke 12:16-21). No matter how much you earn, if you try to create happiness by accumulating wealth, you will never have enough. Money in itself is not wrong, but loving money leads to all sort of sin. Whatever your financial situation, do not depend on money to make you happy, use what you have for the Lord.

God wants us to view what we have with the right perspective—our possessions are a gift from God. Although they are not the source of joy, they are a reason to rejoice because everything good comes from God. We should focus more on the Giver than the gift.

We can be content with what we have when we realize that in God we have everything we need.

CHAPTER 6:1-12

Now, Solomon shows that having the right attitude about God can help us deal with the present injustices. Prosperity is not always good, and adversity is not always bad. But God is always good; if we live as he wants us to, we will be content.

In verses 3-6, this person has died without being able to enjoy his wealth and honor. Even if he had lived a long life, it is ultimately meaningless in itself because all that he has accumulate is left behind. Everyone dies, and both rich and poor end up in the grave. Many people work hard to prolong life and improve their physical condition. Yet people spend little time or effort on their spiritual health. How shortsighted it is to work hard to extend this life and not take the time to prepare for eternity.

God knows and directs everything that happens, and he is in complete control over our lives, even though at times is may not seem like it. How foolish it is for us to contend with our Creator, who knows us completely and can see the future. (Jeremiah 18:6; Romans 9:19-24).

Solomon is stating the profound truth that we cannot predict what the future holds. The only one who knows what will happen after we are gone is God. No human knows the future, so each day must be lived for its own value. Solomon is arguing against the notion that human Beings can take charge of their own destiny.

In all our plans we should look up to God, not just ahead to the future.

CHAPTER 7:1-29

This seems to contradict Solomon's previous advice to eat, drink, and find satisfaction in one's work—to enjoy what God has given. We are to enjoy what we have while we can but realize that adversity also strikes. Adversity reminds us that life is short, teaches us to live wisely, and refines our character. Christianity and Judaism see value in suffering and sorrow. The Greeks and Romans despised it; Eastern religions seek to live above it; but Christians and Jews see it as a refining fire. Most would agree that we learn more about God from difficulties than from happy times. Do you try to avoid sorrow and suffering at all cost? See your struggles as great opportunities to learn from God.

Many people avoid thinking about death, refuse to face it, and are reluctant to attend funerals. Solomon is not encouraging us to think morbidly, but he knows that it is helpful to think clearly about death. It reminds us that there is still time for change, time to examine the direction of our life, and time to confess our sins and find forgiveness from God. Because everyone will eventually die, it makes sense to plan ahead to experience God's mercy rather than his justice. Money talks, and it can confuse those who would otherwise judge fairly. We hear about bribes given to judges, police officers, and witnesses. Bribes are given to hurt those who tell the truth and help those who oppose it. The person who is involved in extortion or takes a bribe is indeed a fool, no matter how wise he thought he was beforehand. It is said that everyone has a price, but those who are truly wise cannot be bought at any price.

To finish what we start takes hard work, wisdom, self-discipline, and patience. Anyone with a vision can start a big project. But vision without wisdom often results in unfinished projects and goals.

God allows both good times and bad times to come to everyone. He blends them in our lives in such a way that we cannot predict the future or count on human wisdom and power. In good times, we usually give ourselves the credit and in bad times, we tend to blame God without thanking him for the good that comes out of it.

When life appears certain and controllable, do not let self-satisfaction or complacency make you too comfortable, or God may allow bad times to drive you back to him. When life seems uncertain and uncontrollable, do not despair—God is in control and will bring good results out of the tough times.

How can a person be too good or too wise? This is a warning against pride—legalism or false righteousness. Solomon was saying that some people become so good or wise in their own eyes that they become deluded by their own religious acts. They are so rigid or narrow in their views that they lose their sensitivity to the true reason for being good—to honor God. Balance is important. God created us to be whole people who seek his righteousness and goodness. Thus, we should avoid both extremes of legalism and immorality. Solomon, the wisest man in the world, confessed how difficult it had been to act and think wisely. He emphasized that no matter how much we know, there are always mysteries we will never understand. So, thinking you have wisdom is a sure sign that you do not.

Did Solomon think women were not capable of being upright, wise, and good? No, because in the book of Proverbs he personified wisdom as a responsible woman.

The point of Solomon's statement is not that women are unwise, but that hardly anyone, man, or woman, is upright before God. In his search, Solomon found that goodness and wisdom were almost as scarce among men as among women, even though men were given a religious education program in his culture and women were not. In effect, the verse is saying, "I have found only one in a thousand people who is wise in God's eyes. No, I have found even fewer than that!"

CHAPTER 8:1-17

Wisdom is the ability to see life from God's perspective and then to know the best course of action to take. Most people would agree that wisdom is a valuable asset, but how can we acquire it? Proverbs 9:10 teaches that the fear of the Lord (respect and honor) is the beginning of wisdom. Wisdom comes from knowing and trusting God. It is not merely the way to find God. Knowing God will lead to understanding and then to sharing this knowledge with others.

Verse 10 probably refers to how we quickly forget the evil done by others after they have died. Returning from the cemetery, we praise them in the very city where they did their evil deeds!

If God does not punish us immediately for sin, we must not assume that he does not care or that sin has no consequences. When a child does something wrong and is not punished, it is much easier for the child to repeat the act. Remember, God knows every wrong we commit, and one day we will have to answer for all that we have done.

Solomon recommends the remedy for life's unanswered questions, joy, and contentment. We must accept each day with its measure of work, food, and pleasure. Let us learn to enjoy what God has given to refresh and strengthen us so we may continue his work.

Even if he had access to all the world's wisdom, the wisest man would know very little. No one can fully comprehend God and all that he has done, and there are always more questions than answers. But the unknown should not cast a shadow over our joy, faith, or work because we know that someone greater is in control and that we can put our trust in him. Do not let what you do not know about the future destroy the joy God wants to give you today.

CHAPTER 9:1-18

"The same destiny ultimately awaits everyone" means that all will die. When Solomon says that the dead know nothing and that there is no work, planning, knowledge, or wisdom after death, he is not contrasting life with afterlife, but life with death. After you die you cannot change what you have done. Resurrection to a new life after death was a vague concept for Old Testament believers. It was only made clear after Jesus rose from the dead.

Considering the uncertainties of the future and the certainty of death, Solomon recommends enjoying life as God's gift. He may have been criticizing those who put off all present pleasures in order to accumulate wealth, much like those who get caught up in today's rat race. Solomon asks, "What is our wealth really worth anyway?" Because the future is so uncertain, we should enjoy God's gifts while we are able.

Solomon also wrote a proverb about marriage. "The man who finds a wife finds a treasure and receives favor from the Lord" (Proverbs 18:22). How sad it would be to be married and not appreciate or enjoy the companion God has given you.

It is not difficult to think of cases where the fastest and the strongest do not win, the wise are poor, and the skillful are unrewarded with wealth or honor. Some people see such examples and call life unfair, and they are right. The world is finite, and sin has twisted life, making it what God did not intend.

Solomon is trying to reduce our expectations. The book of Proverbs emphasizes how life would go if everyone acted fairly; Ecclesiastes explains what usually happens in our sinful and imperfect world. We must keep our perspective. Do not let the inequities of life keep you from earnest, dedicated work. We serve God, not people (Colossians 3:23).

Our society honors wealth, attractiveness, and success above wisdom. Yet, wisdom is a greater asset than strength, although it is often overlooked. Even though it is more effective, wisdom from people who are poor often goes unheeded. From this parable we can learn to appreciate wisdom, no matter whom it comes from.

Ecclesiastes

CHAPTER 10:1-20

This Proverb has implications for employer/employee relationships. Employees should ride out the temper tantrums of their employer. If we quietly do our work and do not get upset, the employer will probably get over his or her anger and calm down.

By describing these circumstances that are not fair or do not make sense, Solomon is saying that wealth alone cannot bring justice. Solomon continues to build to his conclusion that everything we have from wisdom to riches is nothing without God. But when God uses what little we have, it becomes all we could ever want or need. Trying to do anything without the necessary skills or tools is like chopping wood with a dull ax. Similarly, if you lack skills, you should sharpen them through training and practice, "Sharpening the blade" means recognizing where a problem exists, acquiring or honing the skills or tools to do the job better, and then going out and doing it. Find the areas of your life where your "ax" is dull and sharpen your skills so you can be more effective for God's work.

When the Israelites had immature and irresponsible leaders, their nation fell. The books of 1 and 2 Kings describe the decline of the kingdoms when the leaders were concerned only about themselves. Verses 16-18 here pinpoint the basic problems of these leaders—selfishness and laziness.

Government leaders, businesses, families, even churches get trapped into thinking money is the answer to every problem. We throw money at our problems. But just as the thrill of wine is only temporary, the soothing effect of the last purchase soon wears off, and we have to buy more. Scripture recognizes that money is necessary for survival, but it warns against the love of money, Matthew 6:24; 1 Timothy 6:10; Hebrews 13:5. Money is dangerous because it deceives us into thinking that wealth is the easiest way to get everything we want. The love of money is sinful because we trust money rather than God to solve our problems. Those who pursue its empty promises will one day discover that they have nothing because they are spiritually bankrupt.

CHAPTER 11:1-10

In these verses, Solomon summarizes that life involves both risk and opportunity. Because life has no guarantees, we must be prepared. "Give generously" because life has opportunities and we must seize them. Solomon does not support a stingy, despairing attitude. Just because life is uncertain does not mean we should do nothing. We need a spirit of trust and adventure, facing life's risks and opportunities with God-directed enthusiasm and faith.

Waiting for perfect conditions will mean inactivity. This practical insight is especially applicable to our spiritual life. If we wait for the perfect time and place for personal Bible reading, we will never begin. If we wait for a perfect church, we will never join. If we wait for the perfect ministry, we will never serve. Take steps now to grow spiritually. Do not wait for conditions that may never exist.

Solomon is no dreary pessimist in 11:7–12:14. He encourages us to rejoice in every day but to remember that eternity is far longer than a person's life span. Psalm 90:12 says, "Teach us to make the most of our time, so that we may grow in wisdom." The wise person does not just think about the moment and its impact; he or she takes the long-range view toward eternity. Approach your decisions from God's perspective—consider their impact 10 years from now and into eternity. Live with the attitude that although our life is short, we will live with God forever.

We often hear people say, "It doesn't matter," But many of your choices will be irreversible—they will stay with you for a lifetime. What you do when you are young does matter. Enjoy life now, but do not do anything physically, morally, or spiritually that will prevent you from enjoying life when you are old.

CHAPTER 12:1-14

A life without God can produce bitterness, loneliness, and hopelessness in old age. A life centered around God is fulfilling and can be richer and more bearable when we are faced with disabilities, sickness or handicaps. Being young is exciting. But the excitement of youth can become a barrier to closeness with God if it makes people focus on passing pleasures instead of eternal values. Make your strength available to God when it is still yours—during your youthful years. Do not waste it on evil or meaningless activities that become bad habits and make you callous. Seek God now.

The silver cord, golden bowl, water jar, and pulley symbolize life's fragility. How easily death comes to us; how swiftly and unexpectedly we may return to the dust from which we came. Therefore, we should recognize life as a precious resource to be used wisely and not squandered frivolously.

Stripped of the life-giving spirit breathed into us by God, our bodies return to dust. Stripped of God's purpose, our work is in vain. Stripped of God's love, our service is futile. We must put God first over all we do and in all we do because without him we have nothing. Knowing that life is futile without God motivates the wise person to seek God first.

There is no end of opinions about life and philosophies about how we should live that could be read and studied forever. It is not wrong to study these opinions, but because our life on earth is so short, we should make the best use of time by learning the important truths in God's Word. They affect this life and eternity. Wise students of the Bible will understand and do what it says.

Solomon presents his antidotes for the two main ailments presented in this book. Those who lack purpose and direction in life should fear God and obey his commands. Those who think life is unfair should remember that God will review every person's life to determine how he or she has responded to him, and he will bring every deed into judgment. Have you committed your life to God? Does your life measure up to his standards? The book of Ecclesiastes cannot be interpreted correctly without reading the final verses. No matter what the mysteries and apparent contradictions of life are, we must work toward the single purpose of knowing God.

CONCLUSION

In Ecclesiastes, Solomon shows us that we should enjoy life, but this does not exempt us from obeying God's commands. We should search for purpose and meaning in life, but they cannot be found in human endeavors. We should acknowledge the evil, foolishness, and injustice in life, yet maintain a positive attitude and strong faith in God. Our perspective should be in line with God's perspective.

All people will have to stand before God and be judged for what they have done in this life. We will not be able to use the inequities of life as an excuse for failing to live properly. We need to recognize that human effort apart from God is futile, to put God first—now, to receive everything good as a gift from God, and realize that God will judge every person's life, whether good or evil. How strange that people spend their lives striving for the joy that God gives freely, as a gift.

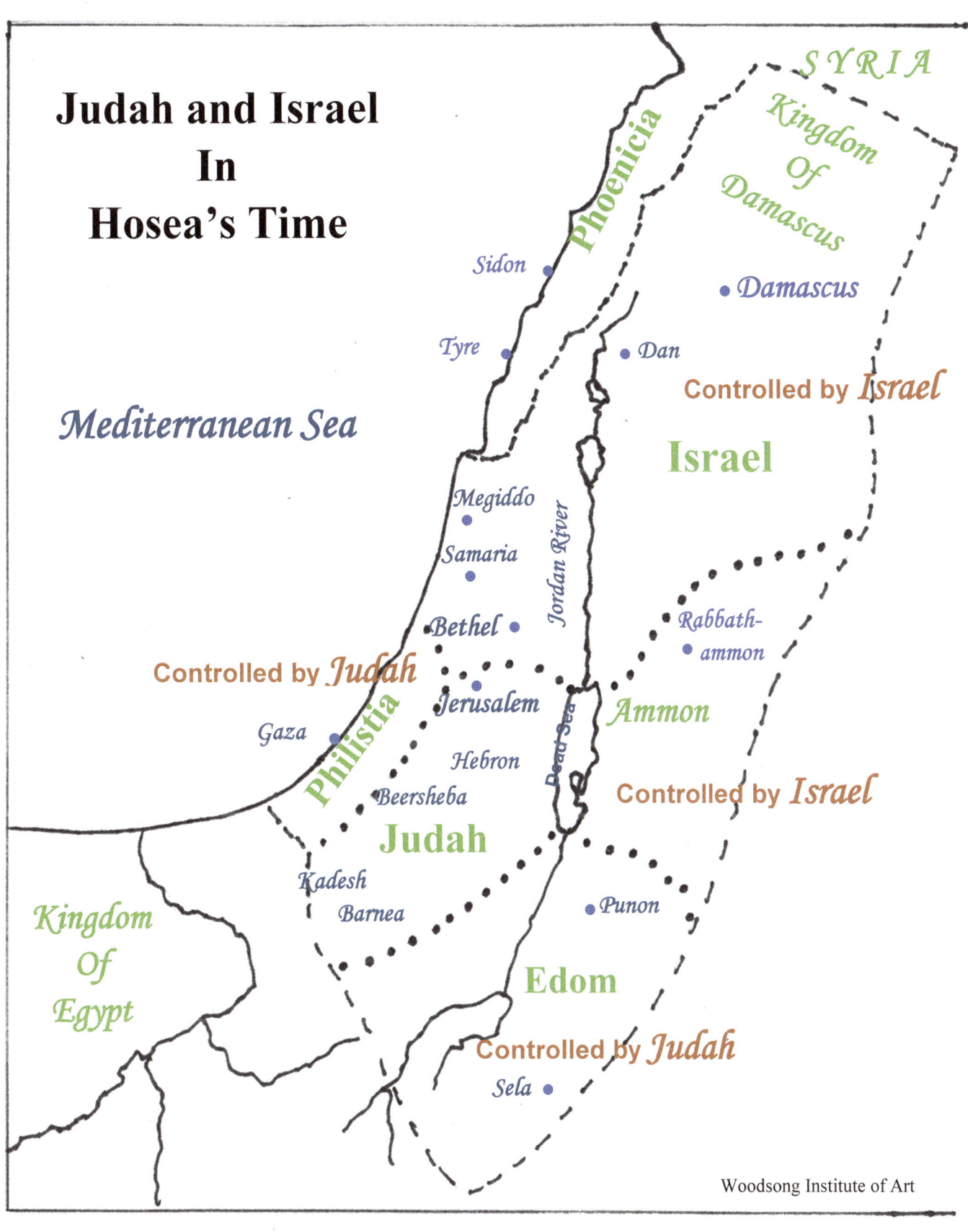

HOSEA

INTRODUCTION

The book of Hosea is a love story—real, tragic, and true. Transcending the tale of a young man, Hosea and his wife, Gomer. It tells of God's love for his people and the response of his "bride." A covenant had been made, and God had been faithful. His love was steadfast, and his commitment unbroken. But Israel, like Gomer, was adulterous and unfaithful, spurning God's love and turning instead to false gods. Then after warning of judgment, God reaffirmed his love and offered reconciliation. His love and mercy were overflowing but justice would be served.

The book dramatically portrays our God's constant and persistent love. As you read this book, watch the prophet submit himself willingly to his Lord's direction; grieve with him over the unfaithfulness of his wife and his people; and hear the clear warning of judgment. Then reaffirm your commitment to being God's person, faithful in your love and true to your vows.

Hosea highlights the parallels between his relationship with Gomer and God's relationship with the nation of Israel. God was merciful toward the people of Israel despite their sins. God has not changed; he is still merciful and forgiving.

CHAPTER 1:1-11

Hosea's wife and Children

Hosea was a prophet to the northern kingdom of Israel. He served from 753 to 715 B.C. Under the reign of Jeroboam II, the northern kingdom had prospered materially but had decayed spiritually. The people there were greedy and had adopted the moral behavior and idolatrous religion of the surrounding Canaanites. Hosea's role was to show how the people of the northern kingdom had been unfaithful to God, their "husband" and provider, and had married themselves to Baal and the gods of Canaan. He warned that unless they repented, of their sin and turned back to God, they were headed for destruction. Hosea spoke of God's characteristics—his powerful love and justice—and how their practical experience of these should affect their lives and make them turn to God. Unfortunately, the people had broken their covenant with God, and they would receive the punishments God had promised (Deuteronomy 27-28).

Did God really order his prophet to marry a woman who was a prostitute? Some who find it difficult to believe God could make such a request view this story as an illustration, not a historical event. Many, however, think this story is historical and give one of these explanations: 1) According to God's law, a priest could not marry a prostitute or a divorced woman (Leviticus 21:7), However, Hosea was not a priest, 2) It is possible that Gomer was not a prostitute when Hosea married her, and that God was letting Hosea know that Gomer would later turn to adultery and prostitution. In any case, Hosea knew ahead of time that his wife would be unfaithful and that their married life would become a living object lesson to the adulterous northern kingdom. Hosea's marriage to an unfaithful woman would illustrate God's relationship to the unfaithful nation of Israel.

It is difficult to imagine Hosea's feelings when God told him to marry a woman who would be unfaithful to him. He may not have wanted to do it, but he obeyed. God often required extraordinary obedience from his prophets who were facing extraordinary times. God may ask you to do something difficult and extraordinary, too. If he does, how will you respond? Will you obey him, trusting that God, who knows everything has a special purpose for his request? Will you be able to accept the fact that the pain involved in obedience may benefit those you serve and not you personally?

Elijah had predicted that the family of Israel's King Ahab would be destroyed because of their wickedness (1 Kings 21:20-22), but Jehu (the son of Jehoshaphat, the tenth King of the northern kingdom of Israel) went too far in carrying out God's command (2 Kings 10:1-11). Therefore, Jehu's dynasty would also be punished—in the Jezreel Valley, the very place where he carried out the massacre of Ahab's family. God's promise to put an end to Israel as an independent kingdom came true 25 years later when the Assyrians conquered the northern kingdom and carried the people into captivity.

In 1:3, we read that Gomer "gave Hosea a son." In 1:6 and 1:8 we learn that Gomer gave birth to two more children, but there is no indication that Hosea was their natural father some translations imply that he was not. The key to this part of the story is found in the names God chose for the children, showing his reaction to Israel's unfaithfulness. God's reaction to unfaithfulness is no different today. He wants our complete devotion.

God said he would personally rescue the people of Judah from their enemies with no help from their weapons or armies. Although God asks us to do our part, we should remember that he is not limited to human effort. God often chooses to work through people, but only because it is good for them. He can accomplish all his purposes without any help from us if he so chooses. You are very important to God, but on your own you have neither the ability to fulfill nor the power to disrupt God's plans.

God was, in essence, dissolving the covenant (Jeremiah 7:23). The name of the third child conveys the finality of God's judgment. God's warnings recorded in Deuteronomy 28:15-68 were beginning to come true. Israel was abandoning God, and in turn, he was leaving them alone and without his blessings.

The Old Testament prophetic books sometimes use the word Israel to refer to the people of the United Kingdom (north and south) and sometimes just to the northern kingdom, in talking about past events. Hosea usually thought of Israel as the northern kingdom with its capital in Samaria. But when Hosea spoke about future events relating to God's promises of restoration, it is difficult to understand his words as applying only to the northern kingdom because the exiled northerners would become hopelessly intermingled with their conquerors. Thus, most scholars see the promises of return as either: 1) conditional—the Israelites chose not to return to God, and therefore they were not entitled to the blessings included in the promise of restoration, or 2) unconditional—God's promises of restoration have been fulfilled in Jesus Christ, and therefore the church (the new Israel) receives his blessings (Romans 9:25-26; 1 Peter 2:10).

Although Israel was unfaithful, God's commitment remained unchanged. This promise of a future reuniting confirmed the covenant made with Moses (Deuteronomy 30:1-10) and foreshadowed the prophecies of Jeremiah (Jeremiah 29:11-14; 31:31-40) and Ezekiel (Ezekiel 11:16-21). It was a prediction of the day when all the people of God will be united under Christ. Today all believers everywhere are God's chosen people, "a kingdom of priests, God's holy nation" (1 Peter 2:9).

Just as the other children's names carried significance so did Jezreel. In verse 4, the name depicts divine judgment; here it represents the scattering. The name means "God scatters." Here it represents the scattering a farmer does when he plants seeds. This was a sign of a new day and a new relationship between God and Israel.

CHAPTER 2:1-23

Charges against an Unfaithful Wife

Israel's punishment and restoration are the themes of this chapter. As in a court case, the prostitute is brought to trial and found guilty. But after her punishment she is joyfully and tenderly restored to God.

The Israelites were thanking false gods (specifically Baal, the god whom they believed controlled weather and thus farming) for their food, shelter, and clothing instead of the true God, who gave those blessings. Therefore, God would fence Israel in "with thorn bushes" and "block the road" by making the rewards of idol worship so disappointing that the people would be persuaded to turn back to God. Despite Israel's unfaithfulness, God was still faithful and merciful. He would continue to hold his arms out to his people, even to the point of placing obstacles in their wayward path to turn them back to him.

Gomer would return to her husband if she thought she would be better off with him, and so, people often return to God when they find life's struggle too difficult to handle. Returning to God out of desperation is better than rebelling against him, but it is better yet to turn to God out of gratitude for his care.

Material possessions are success symbols in most societies. Israel was a wealthy nation at this time, and Gomer may have accumulated silver and gold. But Gomer did not realize that Hosea had given her all she owned, just as Israel did not recognize God as the giver of blessings. Both Gomer and Israel used their possessions irresponsibly as they ran after other lovers and other gods. How do you use your possessions? Use what God has given you to honor him.

The Israelites were so immersed in idolatry that they actually believed pagan gods gave them their vineyards and orchards. They had forgotten that the entire land was a gift from God (Deuteronomy 32:49). Today, many people give credit to everything and everyone but God for their prosperity—luck, hard work, quick thinking, the right contacts. When you succeed, who gets the credit? Baal was the most important of the Canaanite gods, and his name came to be used to describe all the local deities worshiped throughout the land occupied by Israel. Unfortunately, the Israelites did not get rid of the idols and pagan worship centers as they had been commanded. Instead, they tolerated and frequently joined Baal worshipers, often through the influence of corrupt kings. One Israelite king especially noted for his Baal worship was Ahab. The prophet Elijah, in a dramatic showdown with Ahab's hired prophets, proved God's power far superior to Baal's (1 Kings 18).

The Lord's Love for Unfaithful Israel

God was promising (1) to bring the people to the desert, a place free from distractions, so he could clearly communicate with them, and (2) to change what had been a time of difficulty into a day of hope. The Valley of Trouble is the site where Achan (from the tribe of Judah) had sinned by keeping forbidden war plunder (Joshua 7).

He had brought great disaster to Joshua's troops when they were attempting to conquer the land. God uses even our negative experiences to create opportunities to turn back to him. As you face problems and trials, remember that God speaks to you in the "desert" and not just in times of prosperity.

It was not until Judah's exile would the entire nation begin to come to its senses, give up its idols, and turn back to God, and not until that day when God rules through Jesus the Messiah will the relationship between God and his people be restored. In that day, God will no longer be like a master to them; he will be like a husband (Isaiah 54:4-8). The relationship will be deep and personal, the kind of relationship we can know, though imperfectly, in marriage.

The time will come when unfaithfulness will be impossible. God will bind us to himself in his perfect righteousness, justice, love, compassion, and faithfulness. God was promising a fresh new beginning, not just a temporary rewriting of a tired old agreement (Jeremiah 31:31-34).

God's wedding gift to his people both in Hosea's day and in our own, is his compassion. Through no merit of our own, God forgives us and makes us right with him. There is no way for us by our own efforts to reach God's high standards, but he graciously accepts us, forgives us, and draws us into a relationship with himself. In that relationship we have personal and intimate communion with him.

CHAPTER 3:1-5

Hosea's Wife Is Redeemed

This short chapter pictures the nation's exile and return. Israel would experience a time of purification in a foreign land, but God would still love the people and would be willing to accept them back. God commanded Hosea to show the same forgiving spirit to Gomer. Although Hosea had a good reason to divorce Gomer, he was told to buy her back and love her.

Apparently, Gomer was on her own for a while. Needing to support herself, she must have either sold herself into slavery or become the mistress of another man. In either case, Hosea had to pay to get her back—although the required amount was pitifully small. Gomer was no longer worth much to anyone except Hosea, but he loved her just as God loved Israel. No matter how low we sink, God is willing to buy us back—to redeem us—and to lift us up again.

After this, Gomer is no longer mentioned by Hosea. This is explained in verse 4. It is dangerous to rebel against God. If he were ever to withdraw his love and mercy, we would be without hope.

God would separate the Israelites from their treasured idolatrous practices. The sacrifices and temple mentioned were those used for idol worship. The priests served the idols; the idols were household gods, which were strictly forbidden for God's people.

The northern kingdom had rebelled against David's dynasty and had taken Jeroboam as their king (1 Kings

12-13). Their rebellion was both political and religious. At that time, they reverted back to the worship of gold idols. "David's descendant, their king" refers to the time of Messiah's rule when all people will bow before him in humility and submission. Those who will not accept Christ's blessings now will face his power and judgment later. How much better it is to love and follow Christ now than face his angry judgment later.

GOD'S WAYWARD PEOPLE (4:1 – 14:9)

The rest of the book of Hosea deals with Israel's sin and her impending judgment. Hosea points out the moral and spiritual decay of the nation. He describes the punishment awaiting the people and pleads with them to return to God. Although judgment and condemnation of sin are prevalent in the book, a strand of love and restoration runs throughout. Even in the midst of judgment, God is merciful and will restore those who repent and turn to him.

CHAPTER 4: 1-19

Israel's Sinfulness
The Lord's Case against Israel

In this chapter, God brings a charge of disobedience against Israel. The religious leaders had failed to turn the people to God, and ritual prostitution had replaced right worship. The nation had declined spiritually and morally, breaking the laws that God had given them. The people found it easy to condemn Hosea's wife for her adultery. They were not so quick to see that they had been unfaithful to God.

God explained the reasons for Israel's suffering. Their lawless behavior had brought the twin judgments of increased violence and ecological crisis. There is not always a direct cause-and-effect relationship between our actions and the problems we face. Nevertheless, when we are facing difficulties, we should seriously ask, Have I done anything sinful or irresponsible that caused my suffering? If we discover that we are at fault, even partially, we must change our ways before God will help us.

Verse 2 may allude to the assassinations of kings during Hosea's lifetime. Shallum killed Zechariah (the king, not the prophet) and took the throne. Then Menahem killed Shallum and destroyed an entire city because it refused to accept him as king (2 Kings 15:8-16). God pointed out that even murder was being taken casually in Israel. Hosea leveled his charges against the religious leaders.

Who were these religious leaders? When Jeroboam 1 rebelled against Solomon's son Rehoboam and set up a rival kingdom in the north, he also set up his own religious system (1 Kings 12:25-33). In violation of God's law, he made two gold calves and told the people to worship them. He also appointed his own priests, who were not descendants of Aaron. At first the residents of the northern kingdom continued to worship God, even though they were doing it in the wrong way; but very soon they also began to worship Canaanite gods. Before long they had substituted Baal for God and no longer worshiped God at all. It is not surprising that Jeroboam's false priests were unable to preserve the true worship of God.

God accused the religious leaders of keeping the people from knowing him. They were supposed to be spiritual leaders, but they had become leaders in wrongdoing. The people may have said to one another, "it must be ok if the priests do it." Spiritual leadership is a heavy responsibility. Whether you teach a church school class, hold a church office, or lead a Bible study, do not take your leadership responsibilities lightly. Be a leader who leads others to God.

The priests relished the people's sins. Every time a person brought a sin offering, the priest received a portion of it. The more the people sinned, the more the priests received. Because they could not eat all of the offerings themselves, they sold some and gave some to their relatives. The priests profited from the continuation of sin; it gave them power and position in the community.

So instead of trying to lead the people out of sin, they encouraged sin to increase their profits.

The chief Canaanite gods, Baal and Asherah, represented the power of fertility and sexual reproduction. Not surprisingly, their worship included rituals with vile sexual practices. Male worshipers had sex with female temple prostitutes or female priests, and young women wishing to bear children had sex with male priests. But God said their efforts to increase fertility would not succeed.

The "stick," or divining rod, was a way of attempting to tell the future. By divorcing themselves from God's authoritative religion centered in Jerusalem, inhabitants of the northern kingdom had effectively cut themselves off from God's word and from his way of forgiveness. The drive to be free from all restrictions can move us completely out of God's will.

God sent a warning to the southern kingdom of Judah that its priests should not become like those in Israel, (The southern kingdom was called Judah after its most powerful tribe). Israel's priests who remained in the north had forgotten their spiritual heritage and had sold out to Baal. They were promoting idol worship and ritual prostitution. Israel would not escape punishment, but Judah could if it refused to follow Israel's example.

"The mighty wind that would sweep Israel away" refers to the Assyrian invasion that would destroy the nation about 20 years later.

CHAPTER 5:1-15

The Failure of Israel's Leaders

Mizpah and Tabor may have been sites prominent in the false worship of Baal. The leaders likely even encouraged the people into sin at these places. With both their civil and religious leaders hopelessly corrupt, the people of Israel did not have much of a chance. They looked to their leaders for guidance, and they should have found it. Today we can often choose our own leaders, but we still need to be aware of whether they are taking us toward or away from God. God holds us responsible for our actions and choices.

Persistent sin hardens a person's heart, making it difficult to repent. Deliberately choosing to disobey God can sear the conscience; each sin makes the next one easier to commit. Do not allow sin to groove a hard path deep within you. Steer as far away from sinful practices as possible.

Gibeah and Ramah were Israelite cities near Jerusalem. Hosea prophesied that these cities would sound the alarm of the coming judgment.

During the reigns of Menahem and Hoshea, Israel turned to Assyria for help (2 Kings 15:19-20; and 17:3-2). But even the great world powers of that time could not help Israel, for God himself had determined to judge the nation. If we neglect God's call to repentance, how can we escape? (Hebrews 2:3).

CHAPTER 6:1-11

Israel's Punishment; A Call to Repentance

In verses 1-3, this is presumption, not genuine repentance. The people did not understand the depth of their sins. They did not turn from idols, repent of their sins, or pledge to make changes. They thought that God's wrath would last only a few days; little did they know that their nation would soon be taken into exile. Israel was interested in God only for the material benefits he provided; they did not value the external benefits that come from worshiping him. Before judging Israel, however, consider your attitude. What do you hope to gain from your relationship? Do you "repent" easily, without seriously considering what changes need to take place in your life?

God answered his people, pointing out that their profession of loyalty, like mist and dew, evaporated easily and had no substance. Many find it easy and comfortable to maintain the appearance of being committed without deep and sincere loyalty. If you profess loyalty to God, back it up with your actions.

Religious rituals can help people understand God and nourish their relationship with him. That is why God instituted circumcision and the sacrificial system in the Old Testament and baptism and the Lord's Supper in the New Testament. But a religious ritual is helpful only if it is carried out with an attitude of love for and obedience to God. If a person's heart is far from God, ritual will become empty mockery.

God did not want the Israelites' rituals; he wanted their hearts. Why do you worship? What is the motive behind your "sacrifices" and "offerings"?

One of Hosea's key themes is that Israel had broken the covenant God had made with them at Mount Sinai (Exodus 19-20). God wanted to make Israel a blessing and a light to all the nations (Genesis 12:2-3; Isaiah 49:6); and if God's chosen people obeyed him and proclaimed him to the world, he would give them a special blessing. If they broke the covenant, however, they would suffer severe penalties, as they should have known (Deuteronomy 28:15-68). Sadly, the people broke the agreement and proved themselves unfaithful to God. How about you? Have you also broken faith with God? What about your forgotten promises to serve him?

Gilead was once a sacred place, but here it was corrupt. Shechem was once a city of refuge designated by Joshua (Joshua 20:1-2 and 7-8); Gilead was a region that included Ramoth, also a city of refuge. At this time these areas were associated with murder and crime, with bands of evil priests lying in wait to murder travelers passing through the territory.

So that the people of Judah would not become proud as they saw the northern kingdom's destruction, Hosea interjected a solemn warning about God's "harvest." God's Temple was in Judah (Jerusalem), and the people thought that what happened in Israel could never happen to them. But when they had become utterly corrupt, they, too, were led off into captivity (2 Kings 25).

CHAPTER 7: 1-16

Israel's Love for Wickedness

God sees and knows everything. We, like Israel, often forget this. Thoughts like "No one will ever know," or "No one is watching," may tempt us to try to get away with sin. If you are facing difficult temptations, you will be less likely to give in if you remind yourself that God is watching. When faced with the opportunity to sin remember that God sees everything.

"Their hearts blaze like a furnace" refers to the lust for power and intrigue that was burning in these leaders' hearts. Three Israelite kings were assassinated during Hosea's lifetime—Zechariah, Shallum, and Pekahiah (2 Kings 15:8-26). The kings' foreign relations and domestic lives were ruined because they ignored God and his word.

The people of Israel had intermarried with foreign people and had picked up their evil ways. When we spend a lot of time with unbelievers, either professionally or socially, we can easily pick up their attitudes and begin to imitate their actions. Beware of the influence they may have on you. Instead of drifting into bad habits see if you can have a positive influence and point these people to God. Arrogance (pride) keeps a person from turning to God because arrogance claims no need of help from anyone, human or divine. Pride intensifies all our other sins because we cannot repent of any of them without first giving up our pride.

Israel's King Menahem had paid Assyria to support him in power (2 Kings 15:19-20); King Hoshea turned against Assyria and went to Egypt for help (2 Kings 17:4). Israel's kings went back and forth, allying themselves with different nations when they should have allied themselves with God.

A crooked bow is unreliable. Its arrows miss the target, and its owner would be quite vulnerable in battle. Life without God is as unreliable as a crooked bow. Without God's direction, our thoughts are filled with lust, cheating, selfishness, and deceit. As long as we are warped by sin, we will never reach our true potential. People look everywhere except to God for happiness and fulfillment, pursuing possessions, recreation, and relationships. In reality, only God can truly satisfy the deep longings of the soul. Look first to heaven, to the, Most High God. He will meet your Spiritual needs, not all your materialistic wants.

CHAPTER 8:1-14

Israel Harvests the Whirlwind

"The enemy descends like an eagle on the people of the Lord" refers to Assyria coming to attack Israel and take the people into captivity (2 Kings 15:28-29). The people would call to God, but it would be too late because they had stubbornly refused to give up their idols. We, like Israel, often call on God to ease our pain without wanting him to change our behavior. And we, like Israel, may repent after it is too late to avoid the painful consequences of sin.

Samaria was the capital of the northern Kingdom, and sometimes it stands for the whole kingdom of Israel. Jeroboam 1 had set up worship of calf idols at Bethel and Dan and had encouraged the people to worship them (1 Kings 12:25-33). Thus, the people were worshiping the image of a created animal rather than the Creator.

The crop yield is the result of good seed planted in good soil and given the proper proportions of sunlight, moisture and fertilizer. A single seed can produce multiple fruit in good conditions. Israel, however had sown its spiritual seed to the wind—it had invested itself in activities without substance. Like the wind that comes and goes, its idolatry and foreign alliances offered no protection. In seeking self-preservation apart from God, it had brought about its own destruction. Like a forceful whirlwind, God's judgment would come upon Israel by means of the Assyrians.

When we seek security in anything except God, we expose ourselves to great danger. Without God there is no lasting security.

The altars that were supposed to remove sin, were actually increasing sin through their misuse in worshiping Baal. Though the laws were written for them, the people of Israel acted as if those laws did not apply to them. It is easy to listen to a sermon and think of all the people we know who should be listening, or to read the Bible and think of those who should do what the passage teaches. The Israelites did this constantly, applying God's laws to others but not to themselves to avoid making needed changes. As you think of others who need to apply what you are hearing or reading check to see if the same application could fit you. Apply the lessons to your own life first because often our own faults are the very first ones we see in others. In Egypt, the Israelites had been slaves (Exodus 1:11). The people would not literally return to Egypt, but they would return to slavery—this time scattered throughout the Assyrian Empire.

Israel had placed its confidence in military strength, strong defenses, and economic stability, just as nations do today. But because of the people's inner moral decay, their apparent sources of strength were inadequate. There is a tendency in many nations toward removing all traces of God from daily life. But if a nation forgets its Maker, its strengths may prove worthless when put to the test.

CHAPTER 9:1-17

Hosea Announces Israel's Punishment

A threshing floor was a flat area, often built on a hilltop, where harvesters beat the wheat and separated it from the chaff. Often men would stay overnight at the threshing floor to protect their grain, so prostitutes would visit there. Because of the location of the threshing floors in the hilltops, they began to be used as places to sacrifice to false gods.

Israel's leaders vacillated between alliance with Egypt and alliances with Assyria. Hosea was saying that both were wrong. Breaking an alliance with untrustworthy Assyria and fleeing for help to the equally untrustworthy Egypt would not forestall Israel's destruction. Its only hope was to return to God.

By the time Israel began to experience the consequences of its sins it was no longer listening to God's messengers. Refusing to hear the truth from prophets who spoke out so clearly about its sins, the nation did not hear God's warnings about what was soon to happen. We all listen and read selectively, focusing on what seems to support our present life-style and ignoring a radical reordering of our priorities. In doing this, we are likely to miss the warning signs. Listen to people who think your approach is all wrong. Read articles that present viewpoints you would be unlikely to take. Ask yourself, is God speaking to me through these speakers and writers? Is there something I need to change?

A couple had stopped to stay overnight in Gibeah when some wicked men gathered around the house and demanded that the man come out, so they could have sex with him. Instead, the traveler gave them his concubine. They raped and abused her all night and then left her dead on the doorstep (Judges 19:14-30). That horrible act revealed the depths to which the people had sunk. Gibeah was destroyed for its evil (Judges 20:8-48), but Hosea said that the whole nation was now as evil as that city. Just as the city did not escape punishment, neither would the nation.

Baal-Peor was the god of Peor, a mountain in Moab. In Numbers 22, Balaam, a prophet was hired by King Balak of Moab to curse the Israelites as they were coming through his land. The Moabites enticed the Israelites into sexual sin and Baal worship. Before long, the Israelites became as corrupt as the gods they worshiped. People soon begin to copy the characteristics and life-styles of those around them. What do you worship? Are you becoming more like God, or are you becoming more like the world?

At Gilgal, both the political and the religious failure of the nation began. Here idols and kings were substituted for God. Saul, the united nations first king, was crowned at Gilgal (1 Samuel 11:15), but by Hosea's time, Baal worship flourished there (Hosea 4:15; & 12:11).

CHAPTER 10:1-15

The Lord's Judgment against Israel

Israel prospered under Jeroboam II, gaining military and economic strength. But the more prosperous the nation became, the more love it lavished on idols. It seems as though the more God gives, the more we spend! We want bigger houses, better cars, and finer clothes. But the finer things the world offers line the pathway to destruction. As you prosper, consider where your money is going. Is it being used for God's purposes, or are you consuming it all on yourself?

God's anger with the people of Israel for their insincere promises. Because the people did not keep their word, there were many lawsuits. People break their promises, but God always keeps his. Are you remaining true to your promises, both to other people and to God? If not, ask God for forgiveness and help to get back on track. Then be careful about the promises you make. Never make a promise unless you are sure you can keep it.

Beth-aven means "house of wickedness," and it refers to Bethel ("house of God"), where false worship took place. If the Israelites' idols were really gods, they should have been able to protect them. How ironic that the people were fearing for their gods' safety!

In Hosea 9:9 and Judges 19 & 20, you can read more about "that awful night in Gibeah". Gibeah stands for cruelty and sensuality as in Judges, and for rebellion as in Saul's day (Gibeah was Saul's hometown). Hosea repeatedly uses illustrations about fields and crops. Here in verse 12, he envisions a plowed field. It is no longer stony and hard; it has been carefully prepared, and it is ready for planting. Is your life ready for God to work in it? You can break up the unplowed ground of your heart by acknowledging your sins and receiving God's forgiveness and guidance.

The Israelites were taken in by the lie that military power could keep them safe. Believers today sometimes fall for lies. Those who lead others astray often follow these rules: Make it big; keep it simple; repeat it often. Believers can avoid falling for lies by asking 1) Am I believing this because there is personal gain in it for me? 2) Am I discounting important facts? 3) Does this conflict with a direct command of Scripture? 4) Are there any biblical parallels to the situation I am facing that would help me know what to believe?

Some say Shalman was Shalmaneser, king of Assyria; others say Shalman was Salmanu, a Moabite king mentioned in the inscriptions of Tiglath-pileser. Shalman had invaded Gilead around 740 B.C. and destroyed the city of Beth-arbel, killing many people, including women and children. This kind of cruelty was not uncommon in ancient warfare. Hosea was saying such would be Israel's fate. Because Israel had put its confidence in military might rather than in God, it would be destroyed by military power. Israel's king, who had led the people into idol worship, would be the first to fall. Divine judgment is sometimes swift, but it is always sure.

CHAPTER 11:1-12

God's Love for Israel

In the last four chapters, Hosea shifts to the theme of God's intense love for Israel. God had always loved Israel as a parent loves a stubborn child, and that is why he would not release Israel from the consequences of its behavior. The Israelites were sinful, and they would be punished like a rebellious son brought by his parents before the elders (Deuteronomy 21:18-21). All through Israel's sad history God repeatedly offered to restore the nation if it would only turn to him. By stubbornly refusing God's invitation the northern kingdom had sealed its doom. It would be destroyed never to rise again. Even so, Israel as a nation was not finished. A remnant of faithful Israelites would return to Jerusalem, where one day the Messiah would come, offering pardon and reconciliation to all who would faithfully follow him.

God had consistently provided for his people, but they refused to see what he had done, and they showed no interest in thanking him. Ungratefulness is a common human fault. For example, when was the last time you thanked your parents for caring for you? your pastor for the service he gives your church? your child's teacher for the care taken with each day's activities? your heavenly Father for his guidance? Many of the benefits and privileges we enjoy are the result of loving actions done long ago. Look for hidden acts of nurturing and thank those who make the world a better place. But, begin by thanking God for all his blessings.

God's discipline requires times of leading and times of feeding. Sometimes the rope is taut; sometimes it is slack. God's discipline is always loving, and its object is always the well-being of the beloved. When you are called to discipline others—children, students, employees, or church members—do not be rigid. Vary your approach according to the goals you are seeking to accomplish. In each case, ask yourself, does this person need guidance or does he or she need to be nurtured?

The northern kingdom survived for only two centuries after its break with Jerusalem. Its spiritual and political leaders did not help the people learn the way to God, so as a nation they would never repent. Hosea prophesied its downfall, which happened when Shalmaneser of Assyria conquered Israel in 722 B.C. Judah also would go into captivity, but a remnant would return to its homeland.

Admah and Zeboiim were cities of the plain that perished with Sodom and Gomorrah (Genesis 14:8; Deuteronomy 29:23).

"I am God and not a mere mortal." It is easy for us to define God in terms of our own expectations and behavior. In so doing, we make him just slightly larger than ourselves. God is infinitely greater than we are. We should seek to become like him rather than attempt to remake him in our image.

Unlike Israel, Judah had some fairly good kings—Asa, Jehoshaphat, Joash, Amaziah, Aariah, (Uzziah), Jotham and especially Hezekiah and Josiah. Under some of these kings, God's law was dusted off and taught to the people. The priests continued to serve in God's appointed Temple in Jerusalem, and the festivals were celebrated at least some of the time. Unfortunately, the political or religious leaders were unable to completely wipe out idol worship and pagan rites (although Hezekiah and Josiah came close), which continued to fester until they eventually erupted and infected the whole country. Still, the influence of the good kings enabled Judah to survive more than 150 years longer than Israel, and that memory of their positive influence fortified a small group—a remnant—of faithful people who would one day return and restore their land and Temple.

CHAPTER 12:1-14

Jacob, whose name was later changed to Israel, was the common ancestor of all 12 tribes of Israel (both northern and southern kingdoms). Like the nations that descended from him Jacob practiced deceit. Unlike Israel and Judah, however, he constantly searched for God. Jacob wrestled with the angel in order to be blessed, but his descendants thought their blessings came from their own successes. Jacob purged his house of idols (Genesis 35:2), but his descendants could not quit their idol worship.

The two principles that Hosea called his nation to live by, love and justice, are at the very foundation of God's character. They are essential to his followers, but they are not easy to keep in balance. Some people are loving to the point that they excuse wrongdoing. Others are just to the extent that they forget love. Love without justice leaves people in their sins because it is not aiming at a higher standard. Justice without love drives people away from God because it has no heart. To specialize in one at the expense of the other is to distort our witness. Today's church, just like Hosea's nation, must live by both principles.

In Israel, dishonesty had become an accepted means of attaining wealth. Israelites who were financially successful could not imagine that God would consider them sinful. They thought that their wealth was a sign of God's approval, and they did not bother to consider how they had gotten it. But God said that Israel's riches would not make up for its sin.

Remember that God's measure of success is different from ours. He calls us to faithfulness, not affluence. Character is more important to him than our purses.

Rich people and nations often claim that their material success is due to their own hard work, initiative, and intelligence. Because they have bought whatever they wanted, they do not feel the need for God. They believe that their riches are their own and that they have the right to use them any way they please. If you find yourself feeling proud of your accomplishments, remember that all your opportunities, abilities, and resources come from God and that you hold them in sacred trust for him.

Once a year the Israelites spent a week living in tents during the Festival of Shelters, which commemorated God's protection as they wandered in the wilderness for 40 years (Deuteronomy 1:19 – 2:1). Here, because of their sin, God would cause them to live in tents again—this time not as a part of a festival but in actual bondage. Hosea was using this reference to Jacob to say, "Don't forget your humble beginnings. What your have is not a result of your own efforts, but it is yours because God has been gracious to you." The prophet that brought Israel out of Egypt was Moses (Exodus 13:17-19).

CHAPTER 13:1-16

The Lord's Anger against Israel

Israel, represented here by the northern tribe of Ephraim has been great but by Hosea's time the people had rebelled against God and had lost their authority among the nations. Greatness in the past is no guarantee of greatness in the future. It is good to remember what God has done for you and through you, but it is equally important to keep your relationship with him vital and up to date. Commit yourself to God moment by moment.

When abundant possessions made Israel feel self-sufficient, it turned its back on God and forgot him. Self-sufficiency is as destructive today as it was in Hosea's time. Do you see your constant need of God's presence and help? Learn to rely on God, both in good times and bad. If you are traveling along a smooth and easy path right now, beware of forgetting who gave you your good fortune. Do not depend on your gifts; depend on the Giver (Deuteronomy 6:10-12 and 8: 7-20).

God had warned the people of Israel that kings would cause more problems than they would solve, and he reluctantly gave them Saul as their first king (1 Samuel 8:4-22). The second king, David, was a good king, and Solomon, David's son, had his strengths. But after the nation divided in two, the northern kingdom never had another good ruler.

Evil kings led the nations deeper into idolatry and unwise political alliances. Eventually the evil kings destroyed the nation; with Hoshea, the northern kingdom's kings were cut off (2 Kings 17:1-6). Ephraim's (Israel's) sins were recorded for later punishment. All our sins are known and will be revealed at the day of judgment (2 Corinthians 5:10; Revelation 20:11-15).

The apostle Paul used this passage to teach the resurrection of our bodies from death (1 Corinthians 15:55). For those who have trusted in Christ for deliverance from sin, death holds no threat of annihilation.

CHAPTER 14:1-9

Healing for the Repentant

Verses 1-3 are Hosea's call to Repent. Verses 4-8 are God's promise of restoration. God had to punish Israel for its gross and repeated violations of his law, but he would do so with a heavy heart. What God really wanted to do was restore the nation and make it prosper.

The people could return to God by asking him to forgive their sins. The same is true for us; We can pray Hosea's prayer and know our sins are forgiven because Christ died for them on the cross (John 3:16).

Forgiveness begins when we see the destructiveness of sin and the futility of life without God. Then we must admit we cannot save ourselves; our only hope is in God's mercy. When we seek forgiveness, we must recognize that we do not deserve it and therefore we cannot demand it. Our appeal must be for God's love and mercy, not for his justice. Although we cannot demand forgiveness, we can be confident that we have received it because God is gracious and loving and wants to restore us to himself, just as he wanted to restore Israel. "The sacrifice of praise" refers to thank offerings to God. God desired real, heartfelt repentance, not merely annual sacrifices.

When our will is weak, when our thinking is confused, and when our conscience is burdened with a load of guilt, we must remember that God cares for us continually; his compassion never fails. When friends and family desert us, when co-workers do not understand us, and when we are tired of being good, God's compassion never fails. When our shortcomings and our awareness of our sins overcome us, God's compassion never fails.

God's concern for justice that requires faithfulness and for love that offers forgiveness can be seen in his dealings with Hosea. We can err by forgetting God's love feeling that our sins are hopeless; but we can also err by forgetting his wrath against our sins thinking he will continue to accept us no matter how we act. Forgiveness is a key word. When God forgives us, he judges the sin but shows mercy to the sinner. We should never be afraid to come to God for a clean slate and a renewed life.

CONCLUSION

Hosea began his ministry during the end of the prosperous but morally declining reign of Jeroboam II of Israel (the upper classes were doing well, but they were oppressing the poor). He prophesied until shortly after the fall of Samaria in 722 B.C. Hosea employs many images from daily life: God is depicted as husband, father, lion, leopard, bear, dew, rain, moth, and others; Israel is pictured as wife, sick person, vine, grapes, early fruit, olive tree, woman in childbirth, oven, morning mist, chaff, and smoke to name a few.

Hosea closes with an appeal to listen learn, and benefit from God's word. To those receiving the Lord's message through Hosea, this meant the difference between life and death. For you, the reader of the book of Hosea, the choice is similar; you can either listen to the book's message and follow God's way or refuse to walk along the Lord's path. But people who insist on following their own direction without God's guidance are in "complete darkness" and "have no idea what they are stumbling over" (Proverbs 4:19). If you are lost, you can find the way by turning from your sin and following God. True repentance opens the way to a new beginning.

JOEL

The Day of the Lord

. . .Return to the Lord your God, for he is gracious and merciful, slow to anger and abounding in love. Joel 2:13

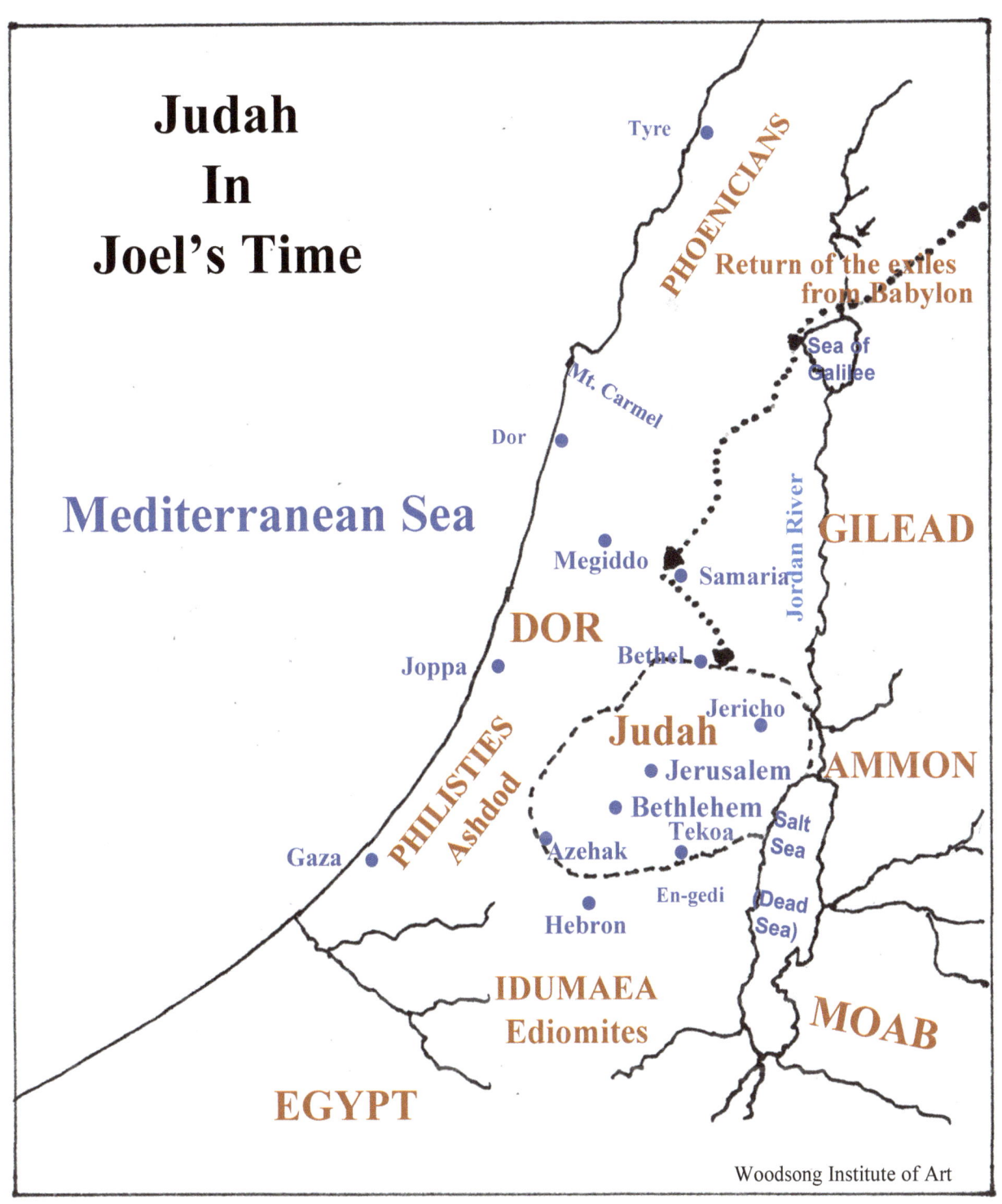

JOEL

INTRODUCTION

Soon the day of the Lord will come! It is about this day that the prophet Joel speaks, and it is the theme of his book. On this day God will judge all unrighteousness and disobedience—all accounts will be settled and the crooked made straight.

We know very little about Joel—only that he was a prophet and the son of Pethuel. He may have lived in Jerusalem because his audience was Judah, the southern kingdom. Whoever he was, Joel speaks forthrightly and forcefully in this short and powerful book. This message is one of foreboding and warning, but it is also filled with hope. Joel states that our Creator, the omnipotent Judge, is also merciful, and he wants to bless all those who trust him.

Joel was a prophet to the nation of Judah, also known as the southern kingdom. The book does not mention when Joel lived, but many believe he prophesied during the reign of King Joash (835-796 B.C.). But the date of Joel's book is not nearly so important as its timeless message. Sin brings God's Judgment; yet with God's judgment there is also great mercy.

Joel begins by describing a terrible plague of locusts that covers the land and devours the crops. The devastation wrought by these creatures is but a foretaste of the coming judgment of God, the "day of the Lord." Joel, therefore, urges the people to turn from their sin and turn back to God. Woven into this message of judgment and the need for repentance is an affirmation of God's kindness and the blessings he promises for all who follow him. In fact, "anyone who calls on the name of the Lord will be saved" (Joel 2:32).

As you read Joel, catch his vision of the power and might of God and of God's ultimate judgment of sin. Choose to follow, obey, and worship God alone as your sovereign Lord.

CHAPTER 1: 1-20

The Day of the Locusts

God urged parents to pass their history down to their children telling over and over the important lessons they learned. One of the greatest gifts you can give young people is your life's story to help them repeat your successes and avoid your mistakes.

A locust plague can be as devastating as an invading army. Locusts gather in swarms too great to number and fly several feet above the ground, seeming to darken the sun as they pass by. When they land, they devour almost every piece of vegetation covering and entering everything in their path.

Joel's detailed description has caused many to believe that he was referring to an actual locust plague that had come or was about to come upon the land. Another view is that the locusts symbolize an invading enemy army. In either case, the locusts represent devastation, and Joel's point was that God would punish the people because of their sin. Joel calls this judgment the "day of the Lord."

The people's physical and moral senses were dulled, making them oblivious to sin. Joel called them to awaken from their complacency and admit their sins before it was too late. Otherwise, everything would be destroyed even the grapes that caused their drunkenness. Our times of peace and prosperity can lull us to sleep. We must never let material abundance hinder our spiritual readiness. Because of the devastation, there was no fine flour or wine for the grain or drink offerings (Leviticus 1).

Sackcloth is the clothing put on by mourners at a funeral. Used here, it would be a sign of repentance.

A fast was a period of time when no food was eaten, and people approached God with humility, sorrow for sin, and urgent prayer. In the Old Testament, people often would fast during times of calamity in order to focus their attention on God and to demonstrate their change of heart and their true devotion (Judges 20:26; 2 Kings 21:27; Ezra 8:21; Jonah 3:5).

The "day of the Lord" is a common phrase in the Old Testament and in the book of Joel. It always refers to some extraordinary happening, whether a present event, an event in the near future, or the final period of history when God will defeat the forces of evil. Even when the day of the Lord refers to a present event, it also foreshadows the final day of the Lord. This final event of history has two aspects to it: 1) the last judgment on all evil and sin and 2) the final reward for faithful believers. Righteousness and truth will prevail, but not before much suffering (Zechariah 14:1-3). If you trust the Lord, looking toward his final day should give you hope, because then all who are faithful will be united forever with God.

Without God, destruction is sure. Those who have not personally accepted God's love and forgiveness will stand before him with no appeal. Be sure to avail yourself to God's love and mercy while you have the opportunity.

CHAPTER 2:1-32

Joel was still describing the devastating effects of the locust plague. The alarm showed that the crisis was at hand. However, Joel implied that the locust plague would be only the forerunner of an even greater crisis if the people did not turn from their sins.

The Garden of Eden was Adam and Eves first home (Genesis 2:8). Known for its beauty, it is used here to describe the beauty of the land prior to the devastation.

God told the people to turn to him while there was still time. Destruction would soon be upon them. Time is also running out for us. Because we do not know when our life will end, we should trust and obey God now while we can. Do not let anything hinder you from turning to him. Deep remorse was often shown by tearing one's clothes. But God did not want an outward display of penitence without true inward repentance. Be sure your attitude toward God is correct, not just your outward actions.

Joel reached a turning point in his message, moving from prophesying about an outpouring of God's judgment to prophesying about an outpouring of God's forgiveness and blessing. But this would come only if the people began to live as God wanted them to, giving up their sins. Where there is repentance, there is hope. This section of the book inspires that hope. Without it, Joel's prophecy could bring only despair. The promise of forgiveness should have encouraged the people to repent. Joel foresaw the invasion from the north by the armies of Assyria and Babylon, typified by the locusts.

Joel contrasts the fear of God's judgment with the joy of God's intervention. On the day of the Lord, sin will bring judgment, and only God's forgiveness will bring rejoicing. Unless you repent, your sin will result in punishment. Let God intervene in your life. Then you will be able to rejoice in that day because you will have nothing to fear. Before, there was fasting, plagues, and funeral dirges; then, there will be feasting, harvesting, and songs of praise. When God rules, his restoration will be complete. In the meantime, we must remember that God does not promise that all his followers will be prosperous now. When God pardons, he restores our relationship with him, but this does not guarantee individual wealth. Instead, God promises to meet the deepest needs of those who love him by loving us, forgiving us, giving us purpose in life, and giving us a caring Christian community.

If the Jews would never again experience a disaster like this locust plague, then, how do we explain the captivity in Babylon, the Jews' slavery under the Greeks and Romans, and their persecution under Hitler? It is important not to take these verses out of context. This is still part of the "blessings" section of Joel's prophecy. Only if the people truly repented would they avoid a disaster like the one Joel had described. God's blessings are promised only to those who sincerely and consistently follow him. God does promise that after the final day of judgment, his people will never again experience this kind of disaster (Zechariah 14:9-11; Revelation 21).

Peter quoted this passage (Acts 2:16-21); the outpouring of the Spirit predicted by Joel occurred on Pentecost. While in the past God's Spirit seemed available to kings, prophets, and judges, Joel envisioned a time when the Spirit would be available to every believer. God's Spirit is available today to anyone who calls on the Lord for salvation. These "wonders" would give a hint or a picture of a coming event. The "day of the Lord" is used here as God's appointed time to judge the nations. Judgment and mercy go hand in hand. Joel had said that if the people repented, the Lord would save them from judgment. In this day of judgment and catastrophe, therefore, some will be saved. God's intention is not to destroy but to heal and to save. However, we must accept his salvation, or we will certainly perish with the unrepentant.

CHAPTER 3:1-21

The phrase "at that time" refers to the time when those who call on the Lord will be saved. God will not only bless believers with everything they need; he will also bless them by destroying all evil and ending the pain and suffering on earth. This prophecy had three fulfillments: immediate, ongoing, and final. Its immediate interpretation could apply to King Jehoshaphat's recent battle against several enemy nations, including Moab and Ammon (2 Chronicles 20). Its ongoing fulfillment could be the partial restoration of the people to their land after the exile to Babylon. The final fulfillment will come in the great battle that precedes the Messiah's reign over the earth (Revelation 20:7-9).

The geographic location of the valley of Jehoshaphat is not known, and some suggest it is being used as a symbol for the place where the Lord is to judge. Some think it may be a future valley created by the splitting of the Mount of Olives when the Messiah returns (Zechariah 14:4). The most important fact for us is that the name 'Jehoshaphat' used here means "YEHWEH judges."

Tyre and Sidon were major cities in Phoenicia to the northwest of Israel; Philistia was the nation southwest of Judah. Phoenicia and Philistia were small countries that rejoiced at the fall of Judah and Israel because they would benefit from the increased trade. God would judge them for their wrong attitude.

Jews were sold to Greeks, a pagan and unclean people. Some think that verses 1 and 6 indicate that Joel lived after the captivity in Babylon (586 B.C.), when the Greek culture began to flourish. But archaeological studies have shown that the Greeks were trading with Phoenicia as early as 800 B.C. These places were contemporary with Judah before their captivity.

The "peoples of Arabia' were also referred to as Sabeans who came from Sheba, a nation in southwestern Arabia. One of Sheba's queens had visited Solomon over a century earlier (1 Kings 10:1-13). The Sabeans controlled the eastern trade routes.

Joel described multitudes waiting in the "valley of decision" (the valley of judgment of verses 2 and 12). Billions of people have lived on earth, and every one of them—dead, living, and yet to be born—will face judgment. Look around you. See your friends—those with whom you work and live. Have they received God's forgiveness? Have they been warned about sin's consequences? If we understand the severity of God's final judgment, we will want to take God's offer of hope to those we know.

The last word will be God's, his ultimate sovereignty will be revealed in the end. We cannot predict when that end will come, but we can have confidence in his control over the world's events. The world's history as well as our own pilgrimage, is in God's hands. We can be secure in his love and trust him to guide our decisions.

The picture of this restored land is one of perfect beauty, similar to the Garden of Eden. The life-giving fountain flowing from the Lord's Temple illustrates the blessings that come from God. Those who trust in him will be forever fruitful. (Ezekiel 47:1-12; Revelation 22:1-2).

Egypt and Edom were two of Israel's most persistent enemies. They represent all the nations hostile to God's people. God's promise that they would be destroyed is also a promise that all evil in the world will one day be destroyed.

The word Judah is used to refer to all God's people—anyone who has called on the name of the Lord. There is full assurance of victory and peace for those who trust in God.

CONCLUSION

A single bomb devastates a city, and the world is ushered into a nuclear age. A Split atom—power and force such as we have never seen. At a launch site, rockets roar and a payload is thrust into space. Discoveries dreamed of for centuries are ours as we begin to explore the edge of the universe.

Volcanos, earthquakes, tidal waves, fires, hurricanes, and tornados unleash uncontrollable and unstoppable force. And we can only avoid them and then pick up the pieces. Power, strength and might—we stand in awe at the natural and man-made display. But these forces cannot touch the power of the omnipotent God. Creator of galaxies, atoms, and natural laws, the Sovereign Lord rules all there is and ever will be. How silly to live without him; how foolish to run and hide from him; how ridiculous to disobey him. But we do. Since Eden, we have sought independence from his control, as though we were gods and could control our destiny. And he has allowed our rebellion.

That is why the Lord says, "turn to me now, while there is time! Give me your hearts. Come with fasting, weeping, and mourning. Do not tear your clothing in your grief; instead, tear your hearts. Return to the Lord your God, for he is gracious and merciful. He is not easily angered. He is filled with kindness and is eager not to punish you" (Joel 2:12-13).

Joel began with a prophecy about the destruction of the land and ended with a prophecy about its restoration. He began by stressing the need for repentance and ended with the promise of forgiveness that repentance brings.

Joel was trying to convince the people to wake up, get rid of their complacency, and realize the danger of living apart from God. His message to us is that there is still time; anyone who calls on God's name can be saved.

Those who turn to God will enjoy the blessings mentioned in Joel's prophecy; those who refuse will face destruction.

OBADIAH

INTRODUCTION

Obadiah is the shortest book in the Old Testament. It is a dramatic example of God's response to anyone who would harm his children. Edom was a mountainous nation, occupying the region southeast of the Dead Sea including Petra the spectacular city discovered by archaeologists a few decades ago. As descendants of Esau, the Edomites were blood relatives of Israel, and like their father, they were rugged, fierce, and proud warriors with a seemingly invincible mountain home. Of all the people, they should have rushed to the aid of their northern brothers. Instead, however, they gloated over Israel's problems, captured and delivered fugitives to the enemy, and even looted Israel's countryside.

Obadiah gave God's message to the Edomites. Because of their indifference to and defiance of God, their cowardice and pride, and their treachery toward their brothers in Judah, they stood condemned and would be destroyed. The book begins with the announcement that disaster is coming to Edom. This concise prophecy ends with a description of the "day of the Lord," when judgement will fall on all who have harmed God's people.

CHAPTER 1:1-21

Edom's destruction

Obadiah was a prophet from Judah who told of God's judgment against the nation of Edom. There are two commonly accepted dates of this prophecy: 1) between 853 and 841 B.C., when King Jehoram and Jerusalem were attacked by a Philistine/Arab coalition (2 Chronicles 21:16); and 2) 586 B.C., when Jerusalem was completely destroyed by the Babylonians (2 Kings 25; & 2 Chronicles 36). Edom had rejoiced over the misfortunes of both Israel and Judah, and yet the Edomites and Jews descended from two brothers—Esau and Jacob (Genesis 25:19-26). But just as these two brothers were constantly fighting so were Israel and Edom. God pronounced judgment on Edom for its callous and malicious actions toward his people.

Edom was Judah's southern neighbor, sharing a common boundary. But neighbors are not always friends, and Edom liked nothing about Judah. Edom's capital at this time was Sela (perhaps the later city of Petra), a city considered impregnable because it was cut into rock cliffs and set in a canyon that would be entered only through a narrow gap. What Edom perceived as its strengths would be its downfall: 1) safety in their city (v. 1-4)—God would send them plummeting from the heights; 2) pride in their self-sufficiency (v.4)—God would humble them; 3) wealth (v. 5-6)—thieves would steal all they had; 4) allies (v. 7)—God would cause them to turn against Edom; 5) wisdom (v. 8-9)—the wise would be destroyed. The Edomites felt secure, and they were proud of their self-sufficiency. But they were fooling themselves because there is no lasting security apart from God. Is your security in objects or people? Ask yourself how much lasting security they really offer. Possessions and people can disappear in a moment, but God does not change, only he can supply true security.

The Edomites were proud of their city carved right into the rock. Today Sela, or Petra, is considered one of the marvels of the ancient world, but only as a tourist attraction. The Bible warns that pride is the surest route to self-destruction (Proverbs 16:18). Just as Petra and Edom fell, so will proud people fall. A humble person is more secure than a proud person because humility gives a more accurate perspective of oneself and the world.

God did not pronounce these harsh judgments against Edom out of vengeance but in order to bring about justice. God is morally perfect and demands complete justice and fairness. The Edomites were simply getting what they deserved. Because they robbed, they would be robbed. Because they took advantage of others, they would be used. Do not talk yourself into sin, thinking that "nobody will know" or "I won't get caught." God knows all our sins, and he will be just.

Edom was noted for its wise men. There is a difference, however, between human wisdom and God's wisdom. The Edomites may have been wise in the ways of the world, but they were foolish because they ignored and even mocked God.

Eliphaz, one of Jobs three friends (Job 2:11), was from

Teman, about five miles east of Petra. Teman was named after Esau's grandson (Genesis 36:11).

The Israelites descended from Jacob, and the Edomites from his brother Esau (Genesis 25:19-26). Instead of helping Israel and Judah when they were in need, Edom allowed them to be destroyed and even plundered what was left behind. Edom, therefore acted like a stranger and it would be punished. Anyone who does not help God's people is God's enemy. If you have withheld your help from someone in a time of need, this is sin (James 4:17). Sin includes not only what we do, but also what we refuse to do. Do not ignore or refuse to help those in need.

The Edomites were glad to see Judah in trouble. Their hatred made them want the nation destroyed. For their wrong attitudes and actions, God wiped out the Edomites. How often do you find yourself rejoicing at the misfortunes of others? Because God alone is the judge, we must never be happy about others' misfortunes, even if we think they deserve them (Proverb 24:17).

Of all Israel and Judah's neighbors, the Edomites were the only ones not promised any mercy from God. This was because they looted Jerusalem and rejoiced at the misfortunes of Israel and Judah. They betrayed their blood brothers in times of crises and aided their brother's enemies.

Edom destroyed, Israel Restored

Why will God's judgment fall on all nations? Edom was not the only nation to rejoice at Judah's fall. A nation and individuals will be judged for the way they have treated

God's people. Some nations today treat God's people favorably, while others are hostile toward them. God will judge all people according to the way they treat others, especially believers (Revelation 20:12-13). Jesus talked about this in Matthew 25:31-46.

Israel's Restoration

The Edomites were routed by Judas Maccabeus in 164 B.C. The nation no longer existed by the first century A.D. At the time of Obadiah's prophecy. Edom may have seemed more likely to survive than Judah. Yet Edom has vanished, and Judah still exists. This demonstrates the absolute certainty of God's Word and of the punishment awaiting all who have mistreated God's people.
The Negev was the southern part of Judah, a dry, hot region. The foothills were in the western part of Judah. The boundaries of the kingdom would be extended to include Phoenicia as far north as Zarephath, located between Tyre and Sidon on the Mediterranean coast.
Obadiah brought Gods message of judgment on Edom. God was displeased with both their inward and their outward rebellion. People today are much the same as people in Obadiah's time, filled with arrogance, envy, and dishonesty. We may wonder how much longer evil will continue. Regardless of sin's effects, however, God is in control. Do not despair or give up hope. Know that when all is said and done, the Lord is still sovereign and the confidence you place in him will not be in vain.

CONCLUSION

Edom is an example to all the nations that are hostile to God. Nothing can break God's promise to protect his people from complete destruction. In the book of Obadiah, we see four aspects of God's message of judgment:

1) Evil will certainly be punished
2) Those faithful to God have hope for a new future
3) God is sovereign in human history
4) God's ultimate purpose is to establish his eternal kingdom

The Edomites had been cruel to God's people. They were arrogant and proud, and they took advantage of others' misfortunes. Any nation that mistreats people who obey God will be punished regardless of how invincible they appear. Similarly, we, as individuals, cannot allow ourselves to feel so comfortable with our wealth or security that we do not help God's people. This is sin. And because God is just, sin will be punished.

A Journey with JONAH
The Runaway Prophet

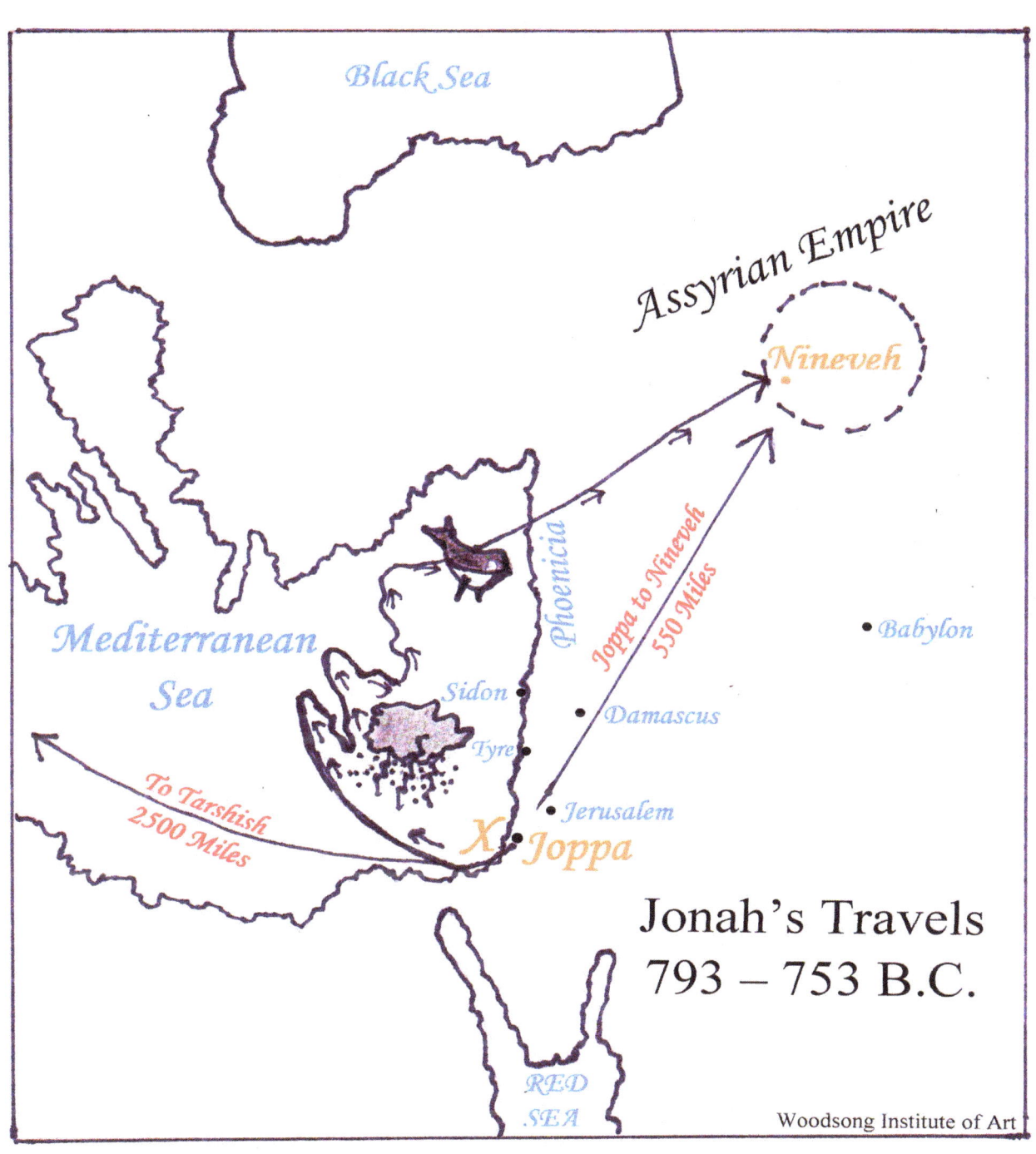

JONAH

INTRODUCTION

Assyria—a great but evil empire—was Israel's most dreaded enemy. The Assyrians flaunted their power before God and the world through numerous acts of heartless cruelty. So, when Jonah heard God tell him to go to Assyria and call the people to repentance, he ran the opposite direction.

The book of Jonah tells the story of this prophet's flight and how God stopped him and turned him around. But it is much more than a story of a man and a great fish. Jonah's story is a profound illustration of God's mercy and grace. No one deserved God's favor less than the people of Nineveh, Assyria's capital. Jonah knew this. But he knew that God would forgive and bless them if they would turn from their sin and worship him. Jonah also knew the power of God's message, that even through his own weak preaching they would respond and be spared God's judgment. Eventually Jonah obeyed and preached in the streets of Nineveh, and the people repented and were delivered from judgment. Jonah complained to God, and in the end, God confronted Jonah about his self-centered values and lack of compassion.

As you read Jonah, see the full picture of God's love and compassion and realize that no one is beyond redemption.

CHAPTER 1:1-17

Jonah forsakes his mission and runs from the Lord

Jonah is mentioned in 2 Kings 14:25 and he prophesied during the reign of Jeroboam II, the king of Israel from 793 to 753 B.C. He may have been a member of the company of prophets mentioned in connection with Elisha's ministry (2 Kings 2:3).

God told Jonah to preach to Nineveh, the most important city in Assyria, the rising world power of Jonah's day. Within 50 years, Nineveh would become the capital of the vast Assyrian Empire. Jonah does not say much about Nineveh's wickedness, but the prophet Nahum gives us more insight. Nahum says that Nineveh was guilty of 1) evil plots against God; 2) exploitation of the helpless; 3) cruelty in war; and 4) idolatry, prostitution, and witchcraft. God told Jonah to go to Nineveh, about 500 miles northeast of Israel, to warn of judgment and to declare that the people could receive mercy and forgiveness if they repented.

Nineveh was a powerful and wicked city. Jonah had grown up hating the Assyrians and fearing their atrocities. His hatred was so strong that he did not want them to receive God's mercy. Jonah was actually afraid that the people would repent. Jonah's attitude is representative of Israel's reluctance to share God's love and mercy with others, even though this was their God-given mission (Genesis 12:3). They, like Jonah, did not want non-Jews (Gentiles) to obtain God's favor. Jonah knew that God had a specific job for him, but he did not want to do it. Tarshish could be one of any number of Phoenicia's western ports. Nineveh was toward the east. Jonah decided to go as far west as he could. When God gives us directions through his Word, sometimes we run in fear or in stubbornness, claiming that God is asking too much. It may have been fear or anger at the wideness of God's mercy that made Jonah run. But running got him into worse trouble. In the end, Jonah understood that it is best to do what God asks in the first place. But by then he had paid a costly price for running. It is far better to obey from the start.

Before settling in the Promised Land, the Israelites had been nomads, wandering from place to place, seeking good pastureland for their flocks. Although they were not a seafaring people, their location along the Mediterranean Sea and near the neighboring maritime powers of Phoenicia and Philistia allowed much contact with ships and sailors. The ship Jonah sailed on was probably a large trading vessel with a deck. Jonah's disobedience to God endangered the lives of the ship's crew. We have a great responsibility to obey God's Word because our sin and disobedience can hurt others around us.

While the storm raged, Jonah was sound asleep below deck. Even as he ran from God, Jonah's actions apparently did not bother his conscience. But the absence of guilt is not always a barometer of whether we are doing right. Because we can deny reality we cannot measure obedience by our feelings. Instead, we must compare what we do with God's standards for living.

The crew cast lots to find the guilty person, relying on their superstition to give them the answer. Their system worked, but only because God intervened to let Jonah know that he could not run away.

We cannot seek God's love and run from him at the same time. Jonah soon realized that no matter where he went, he could not get away from God. But before Jonah could return to God, he first had to stop going in the opposite direction. What has God told you to do? If you want more of God's love and power, you must be willing to carry out the responsibilities he gives you. You cannot say that you truly believe in God if you do not do what he says (1 John 2:3-6). Jonah knew that he had disobeyed and that the storm was his fault, but he did not say anything until the crew cast lots and he lost the toss. Then Jonah was willing to give his life to save the sailors, although he had refused to do the same for the people of Nineveh. Jonah's hatred for the Assyrians had affected his perspective.

By trying to save Jonah's life, the pagan sailors showed more compassion than Jonah, because Jonah did not want to warn the Ninevites of the coming judgment of God. Believers should be ashamed when unbelievers show more concern and compassion than they do. God wants us to be concerned for all of his people, lost, and saved.

Jonah had disobeyed God, but, while he was running away, he stopped and submitted to God. Then the ship's crew began to worship God because they saw that the storm had stopped. God is able to use even our mistakes to help others come to know him. It may be painful but, admitting our sins can be a powerful example to those who do not know God. Ironically, the pagan sailors did what the entire nation of Israel would not do—prayed to God and vowed to serve him.

Many have tried to dismiss this miraculous event as fiction, but the Bible does not describe it as a dream or a legend. We should not explain away this miracle as if we could pick and choose which of the miracles in the Bible we believe and which ones we do not. That kind of attitude would allow us to question any part of the Bible and cause us to lose our trust in the Bible as God's true and reliable Word. Jonah's experience was used by Christ himself as an illustration of his death and resurrection (Matthew 12:39-40).

CHAPTER 2:1-10

Jonah's Prayer

Jonah's prayer is one of thanksgiving, not a prayer for deliverance. Jonah was simply thankful that he had not drowned. Jonah pictured his predicament inside the belly of the fish as though he had been buried alive. He was delivered in a most spectacular way and was overwhelmed that he had escaped certain death. Even from the inside the fish, Jonah's prayer was heard by God. We can pray anywhere and at any time, even in the darkest of our struggle, and God will hear us. Your sin is never too great, your predicament never too difficult, for God.

Jonah said, "When I lost all hope, I turned my thoughts once more to the LORD." Often, we act the same way. When life is going well, we tend to take God for granted; but when we lose hope, we cry out to him. This kind of relationship with God can result only in an inconsistent, up-and-down spiritual life. A consistent, daily commitment to God promotes a solid relationship with him. Look to God during both the good and bad times, and you will have a stronger spiritual life.

Those who worship worthless idols forfeit God's grace and abandon any hope for mercy from the Lord. Any object of our devotion that replaces God is a lying vanity. We deceive ourselves with something that is ultimately empty and foolish. Make sure that nothing takes God's rightful place in your life.

Obviously, Jonah was not in a position to bargain with God. Instead, he simply thanked God for saving his life. Our troubles should cause us to cling tightly to God, not attempt to bargain our way out of the pain. We can thank and praise God for what he has already done for us, and for his love and mercy. It took a miracle of deliverance to get Jonah to do as God had commanded. As a prophet, Jonah was obligated to obey God's Word, but he had tried to escape his responsibilities. At this time, he pledged to keep his vows. Jonah's story began with a tragedy, but a greater tragedy would have happened if God had allowed him to keep running. When you know God wants you to do something, do not run. God may not stop you as he did Jonah.

CHAPTER 3:1-10

Jonah fulfills his mission and goes to Nineveh

Jonah had run away from God but was given a second chance to participate in God's work. You may feel as though you are disqualified from serving God because of past mistakes. But serving God is not an earned position. No one qualifies for God's service, but God still asks us to carry out his work. You may yet have another chance. Jonah was to preach only what God told him—a message of doom to one of the most powerful cities in the world. This was not the most desirable assignment, but those who bring God's word to others should not let social pressures or fear of people dictate their words. They are called to preach God's message and his truth, no matter how unpopular it may be.

Nineveh was a huge city. The Hebrew text makes no distinction between the city proper (the walls of which were only about eight miles in circumference, accommodating a population of about 175,000 people) and the administrative district of Nineveh that was about 30-60 miles across.

God's Word is for everyone. Despite the wickedness of the Ninevite people, they were open to God's message and repented immediately. If we simply proclaim God's message of salvation, we may be surprise at how many people will listen. The pagan people of Nineveh believed Jonah's message and repented. What a miraculous effect God's words had on those evil people! Their repentance stood in stark contrast to Israel's stubbornness. The people of Israel had heard many messages from the prophets, but they had refused to repent. The people of Nineveh only needed to hear God's message once. Jesus said that at the judgment, the people of Nineveh will stand up to condemn the Israelites for their failure to repent. It is not our hearing God's Word that pleases him, but our responding obediently to it. God responded in mercy by canceling his threatened destruction. God had said that any nation on which he had pronounced judgment would be saved if it repented (Jeremiah 18:7-8). God forgave Nineveh, just as he had forgiven Jonah. The purpose of God's judgment is correction, not revenge. He is always ready to show compassion to anyone willing to seek him.

CHAPTER 4:1-11

Jonah's anger at the Lord's Mercy

Jonah became angry when God spared Nineveh. The Jews did not want to share God's message with Gentile nations in Jonah's day, just as they resisted that role in Paul's day (1 Thessalonians 2:14-16). They had forgotten their original purpose as a nation—to be a blessing to the rest of the world by sharing God's message with other nations. Jonah thought that God should not freely give his salvation to a wicked pagan nation. Yet this is exactly what God does for all who come to him today in faith. Jonah revealed the reason for his reluctance to go to Nineveh: he did not want the Ninevites forgiven; he wanted them destroyed. Jonah did not understand that the God of Israel was also the God of the whole world. Are you surprised when some unlikely person turns to God? Is it possible that your view is as narrow as Jonah's? We must not forget that, in reality we do not deserve to be forgiven by God.

Jonah had run from the job of delivering God's message of destruction to Nineveh; then he wanted to die because the destruction would not happen. How quickly Jonah had forgotten God's mercy for him when he was inside the belly of the fish. Jonah was happy when God saved him, but he was angry when Nineveh was saved. But Jonah was learning a valuable lesson about God's mercy and forgiveness. God's forgiveness was not only for Jonah or for Israel alone, it extends to all who repent and believe. Jonah may have been more concerned about his own reputation than God's. He knew that if the people repented none of his warnings to Nineveh would come true. This would embarrass him, although it would give glory to God. Are you more interested in getting glory for God or for yourself?

God ministered tenderly to Jonah just as he had done to Nineveh and to Israel—and just as he does to us. God could have destroyed Jonah for his defiant anger, but instead he gently taught him a lesson. If we will obey God, he will lead us. His harsh judgment is reserved for those who persist in rebellion.

Jonah was angry at the withering of the plant, but not over what could have happened to Nineveh. Most of us have cried at the death of a pet or when an object with sentimental value is broken, but have we cried over the fact that a friend does not know God? How easy it is to be more sensitive to our own interests than to the spiritual needs of people around us.

Sometimes people wish that judgment and destruction would come upon sinful people whose wickedness seems to demand immediate punishment. But God is more merciful than we can imagine. God feels compassion for the sinners we want judged and he devises plans to bring them to himself. What is your attitude toward those who are especially wicked? Do you want them destroyed? Or do you wish that they could experience God's mercy and forgiveness?

CONCLUSION

Sin runs rampant in society—daily headlines and overflowing prisons bear dramatic witness to that fact. With child abuse, pornography, serial killings, terrorism, anarchy, and ruthless dictatorships, the world seems to be filled to overflowing with violence hatred and corruption.

God spared the sailors when they pleaded for mercy. God saved Jonah when he prayed from inside the fish. God saved the people of Nineveh when they responded to Jonah's preaching. God answers the prayers of those who call upon him. God will always work his will, and he desires that all come to him, trust in him, and be saved. We can be saved if we heed God's warnings to us through his Word. If we respond in obedience, God will be gracious, and we will receive his mercy, not his punishment.

The gospel is for all who will repent and believe. Begin to pray for those who seem to be farthest from the kingdom and look for ways to tell them about God. Learn from the story of this reluctant prophet and determine to obey God, doing whatever he asks and going wherever he leads.

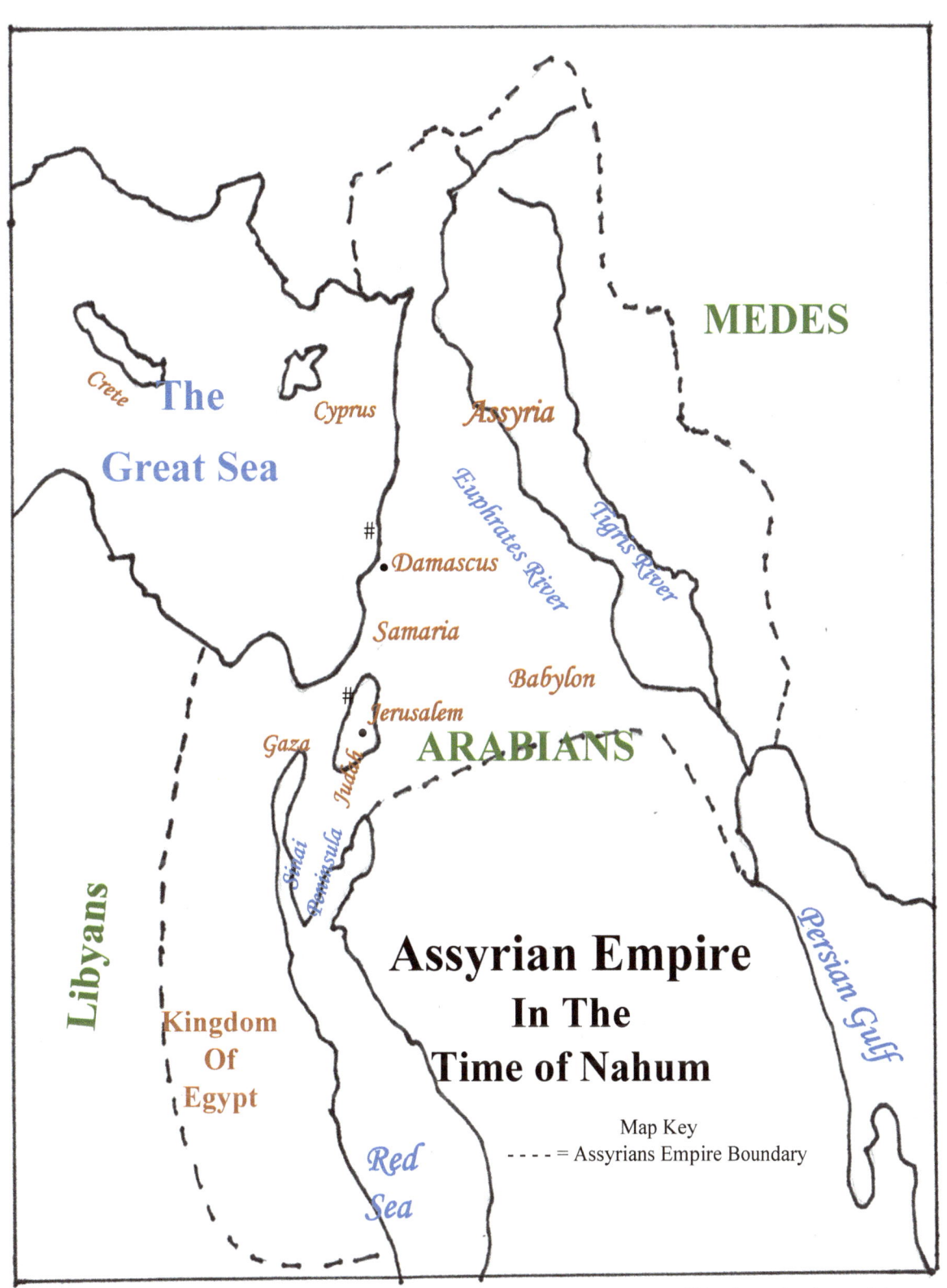

NAHUM

INTRODUCTION

Nahum, like Jonah, was a prophet to Nineveh, the capital of the Assyrian Empire, and he prophesied between 663 and 612 B.C. One hundred years earlier, Jonah had preached in the streets of the great city of Nineveh; the people had heard God's message and had turned from their evil. But generations later, the prophet Nahum pronounced judgment on this wicked nation; that they would be utterly destroyed because of their sins. That end came within 50 years.

Nineveh, the capital of the Assyrian Empire, is the subject of Nahum's prophecy. The news of its coming destruction was a relief for Judah, who was subject to Assyrian domination. Judah was comforted to know that God was still in control. Nineveh is an example to all who are seemingly invincible. We can be confident that God's power and justice will one day conquer all evil.

Assyria was the most powerful nation on earth. Proud in their self-sufficiency and military might, they plundered oppressed, and slaughtered their victims. In this judgment of Assyria and its capital city, Nineveh, God is judging a sinful world. And the message is clear: Disobedience, rebellion and injustice will not prevail but will be punished severely by a righteous and holy God, who rules over all the earth.

As you read Nahum, sense God's wrath as he avenges sin and brings about justice. Then decide to live under his guidance and within his rules, commands, and guidelines for life.

CHAPTER 1:1-15

Nineveh's judge

Jonah had seen Nineveh repent a century earlier, but the city had fallen back into wickedness. Assyria, the world power controlling the Fertile Crescent, seemed unstoppable. Its ruthless and savage warriors had already conquered Israel, the northern kingdom, and were causing great suffering in Judah. So, Nahum proclaimed God's anger against Assyria's evil. Within a few decades, the mighty Assyrian Empire would be toppled by Babylon. Elkosh was a village thought by some to be in southwest Judah.

God alone has the right to be jealous and to carry out vengeance. Jealousy and vengeance may be surprising terms to associate with God. When humans are jealous and take vengeance, they are usually acting in a spirit of selfishness. Their purpose is to remove sin and restore peace to the world (Deuteronomy 4:24; 5:9).

God is slow to get angry, but when he is ready to punish, even the earth trembles. Often people avoid God because they see evildoers in the world and hypocrites in the church. They do not realize that because God is slow to anger, he gives his true followers time to share his love and truth with evildoers. But judgment will come; God will not allow it to go unchecked forever. When people wonder why God does not punish evil immediately, help them to remember that if he did, none of us would be here. We can all be thankful that God gives people time to turn to him.

No person on earth can safely defy God, the Almighty, the Creator of all the universe. God, who controls the sun, the galaxies, and the vast stretches beyond also controls the rise and fall of nations. How could a small temporal kingdom like Assyria, no matter how powerful, challenge God's awesome power? If only Assyria could have looked ahead to see the desolate mound of rubble that it would become—and yet God would still be alive and well! Do not defy God; he will be here forever with greater power than that of all armies and nations combined. To the people who refuse to believe, God's punishment is like an angry fire. To those who love him, his mercy is a refuge supplying all their needs without diminishing his supply. But to God's enemies he is an overwhelming flood that will sweep them away. The relationship we have with God is up to us. What kind of relationship will you choose?

The one "who dares to plot evil against the Lord" could have been 1) Ashurbanipal, King of Assyria during much of Nahum's life and the one who brought Assyria to the zenith of its power; or 2) Sennacherib, who openly defied God, epitomizing rebellion against God; or 3) no one king, but the entire evil monarchy. The point is that Nineveh would be destroyed for rebelling against God.

The good news for Judah whom Assyria afflicted, was that its conquerors and tormentors would be destroyed and would never rise to torment it again. Nineveh was so completely wiped out that its ruins were not identified until 1845.

CHAPTER 2:1-13

This chapter predicts the events of 612 B.C. when the combined armies of the Babylonians and the Medes sacked the seemingly impregnable Nineveh.

Assyria had plundered and crushed the northern kingdom (Israel) and had deported its people in 722 B.C. (2 Kings 17:3-6; 18:9-22). Assyria had also attacked the southern kingdom and had forced it to pay tribute.

The opening of river gates could refer either to the enemy flowing into Nineveh like a flood or to an actual flood of water. Some scholars suggest that dam gates, which were found in archaeological excavations, were closed to dam up the river. When an enormous amount of water had been accumulated, the gates were opened, allowing the water to flood Nineveh.

The major source of wealth for the Assyrian economy was the plunder taken from other nations. The Assyrians had taken the food of innocent people to maintain their luxurious standard of living, depriving others to supply their excesses. Depriving innocent people to support the luxury of a few is a sin that angers God. As Christians we must stand firm against this common but evil practice. God had given the people of Nineveh a chance to repent, which they did after hearing Jonah. But they had returned to their sin, and its consequences were destroying them. There is a point for people, cities, and nations after which there is no turning back; Assyria had passed that point. We must warn others to repent while there is still time.

CHAPTER 3: 1-19

Nineveh had used its beauty, prestige, and power to seduce other nations. Like a harlot, she had enticed them into false friendships. Then when the other nations relaxed, thinking Assyria was a friend, Assyria destroyed and plundered them. Beautiful and impressive on the outside, Nineveh was vicious and deceitful on the inside. Beneath beautiful facades sometimes lie seduction and death. Do not let an attractive institution, company, movement, or person seduce you into lowering your standards or compromising your moral principles.

Thebes was a city in Egypt, the previous world power which stood in the path of Assyria's expansion in the south. The Assyrians conquered Thebes 51 years before this prophecy was given. To Judah, surrounded to the north and south by Assyria, the situation appeared hopeless. But God said that the same atrocities done in Thebes would happen in Nineveh. No power on earth can protect us from God's judgment or be a suitable substitute for his power in our life. Thebes and Assyria put their trust in alliances and military power, but history would show that these were inadequate. Do not insist on learning through personal experience; instead, learn the lessons history has already taught. Put your trust in God above all else.

CONCLUSION

All the nations hated to be ruled by the merciless Assyrians, the nations wanted to be like Assyria—powerful, wealthy, prestigious—and they courted Assyria's friendship. In the same way, we do not like the idea of being ruled harshly, so we do what we can to stay on good terms with a powerful leader. And deep down, we would like to have that kind of power. The thought of being on top can be captivating. But power is seductive, so we should not scheme to get it or hold on to it. Those who lust after power will be powerfully destroyed, as was the mighty Assyrian Empire.

There are laws in the world—boundaries and rules for living established by God. But men and women regularly flaunt these regulations, hiding their infractions or overpowering others and declaring that might make right. God calls this sin—willful disobedience, rebellion against his control or apathy. The truth is, however, that ultimately justice will be served in the world. God will settle all accounts.

A Broken World

For thus saith the LORD of hosts; Yet once, it is a little while, and I will shake the heavens, and the earth, and the sea, and the dry land; Haggai 2:6

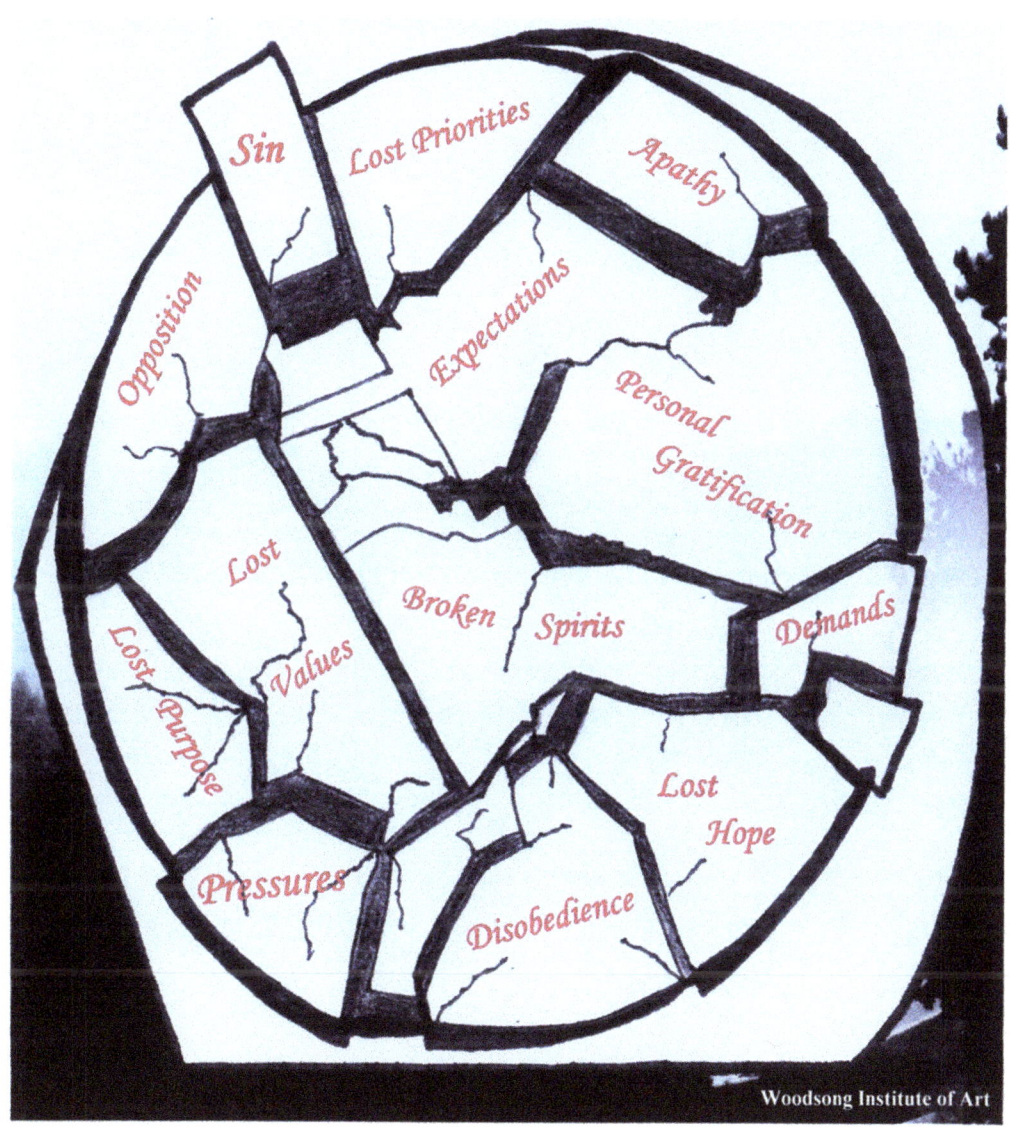

HAGGAI

INTRODUCTION

Our values and priorities are reflected in how we use our resources—time, money, strength, and talent. Often our actions belie our words. We say God is number one, but then we relegate him to a letter or number on our "to do" list. Twenty-five centuries ago, a voice was heard, calling men and women to the right priorities. Haggai knew what was important and what had to be done and he challenged God's people to respond.

In 586 B.C., the armies of Babylon had destroyed the Temple in Jerusalem—God's house, the symbol of his presence. In 538 B.C. King Cyrus decreed that Jews could return to their beloved city and rebuild the Temple. So, they began the work, but then they forgot their purpose and lost their priorities, as opposition and apathy brought the work to a standstill (Ezra 4:4-5).

Although Haggai is a small book, it is filled with challenge and promise, reminding us of God's claim on our life and our priorities. As you read Haggai, imagine him walking the streets and alleys of Jerusalem, urging the people to get back to doing God's work. And listen to Haggai speaking to you, urging you to reorder your priorities in accordance with God's will. What has God told you to do? Put all else aside and obey Him.

CHAPTER 1:1-15

A Call to Rebuild the Temple

Zerubbabel, governor of Judah, and Jeshua the high priest were key leaders in rebuilding the Temple. They had already reestablished the altar, but work on the Temple had slowed. Haggai gave a message on August 29 520 B.C., to these outstanding leaders and to the exiles who had returned from Babylon, encouraging them to complete the rebuilding of the Temple in Jerusalem.

The Jews who had returned from Babylon in 538 B.C. to rebuild the Temple in Jerusalem were not able to finish their work because they were hindered by their enemies. After opposition put a halt to progress, no further work had been done on the Temple for over 15 years. Haggai was probably born in captivity in Babylon and returned to Jerusalem with Zerubbabel in 538 B.C. (Ezra 1-2). Haggai and Zechariah, two prophets who encouraged the Temple rebuilding, are mentioned in Ezra 5:1.

Haggai encouraged the people to finish rebuilding the Temple. Opposition from hostile neighbors had caused them to feel discouraged and to neglect the Temple and thus neglect God. But Haggai's message turned them around and motivate them to pick up their tools and continue the work they had begun.

God asked his people how they could live in luxury when his house was lying in ruins. The Temple was the focal point of Judah's relationship with God, but it was still demolished. Instead of rebuilding the Temple, the people put their energies into beautifying their own homes.

However, the harder the people worked for themselves, the less they had, because they ignored their spiritual lives. The same happens to us. If we put God first, he will provide for our deepest needs. If we put him in any other place, all our efforts will be futile. Caring only for your physical needs while ignoring your relationship with God will lead to ruin.

Because the people had not given God first place in their lives, their work was not fruitful or productive, and their material possessions did not satisfy. While they concentrated on building and beautifying their own homes, God's blessing was withheld because they no longer put him first. Moses had predicted that this would be the result if the people neglected God (Deuteronomy 28:38-45).

Judah's problem was confused priorities. Like Judah, our priorities involving occupation, family, and God's work are often confused. Jobs, homes, vacations, and leisure activities may rank higher on our list of importance than God. What is most important to you? Where is God on your list of priorities?

Grain, grapes for wine, and olives for oil were Israel's major crops. The people depended on these for security while neglecting the worship of God. As a result, God would send a drought to destroy their livelihood and call them back to himself.

Finally, the people began rebuilding the Temple just 23 days after Haggai's first message. Rarely did a prophet's message produce such a quick response. How often we hear a sermon and respond, "That was an excellent point—I ought to do that," only to leave church and forget to act. These people put their words into action. When you hear a good sermon or lesson, ask what you should do about it, and then make plans to put it into practice.

CHAPTER 2:1-23

Encouragement to complete the Temple
The New Temple's Splendor

Chapter 2 gives us Haggai's second message. It was given in October 520 B.C., during the Festival of Shelters. The older people could remember the incredible beauty of Solomon's Temple, destroyed 66 years earlier. Many were discouraged because the rebuilt Temple was inferior to Solomon's. But Haggai encouraged them with God's message that the glory of this Temple would surpass that of its predecessor. The most important part of the Temple is God's presence. Some 500 years later, Jesus Christ would walk in the Temple courts.

"Take courage and work for I am with you." Judah's people had returned to worshiping God, and God had promised to bless their efforts. But it was time for them to work. We must be people of prayer, Bible Study, and worship, but eventually we must get out and do the work God has prepared for us. He wants to change the world through us, his ambassadors. God has given you a job to do in the church, at your place of employment, and at home. The time has come to take courage and get going because God is with you!

The Israelites had been led from captivity in Egypt to their Promised Land. They were God's chosen people, guided and cared for by his Holy Spirit. Although God had punished them for their sins, he kept his promise and never left them (Exodus 29:45).

No matter what difficulties we face or how frustrating our work may be, God's Spirit is with us.

The focus shifts from the local Temple being rebuilt in Jerusalem to the worldwide reign of the Messiah on earth. The words "in just a little while" are not limited to the immediate historical context; they refer to God's control of history—he can act anytime he chooses. God will act in his time (Hebrews 12:26-27).

When God promised to shake all the nations with his judgment, he was speaking of both his present judgment on evil nations and future judgment during the last days. God wanted the Temple to be rebuilt, and he had the gold and silver to do it, but he needed willing hands. God has chosen to do his work through people. He provides the resources, but willing hands must do the work. Are your hands and feet available for God's work in the world?

The point of this message (delivered in December 520 B.C.) is that holiness will not rub off on others, but contamination will. As the people began to obey God, God promised to encourage and prosper them. But they needed to understand that activities in the Temple would not clean up their sin; only repentance and obedience could do that. If we insist on harboring wrong attitudes and sins or on maintaining close relationships with sinful people, we will be defiled. Holy living will come only when we are empowered by God's Holy Spirit.

When a child eats spaghetti, soon his face, hands and clothes are red. Sin and selfish attitudes produce the same result—they stain everything they touch. Even good deeds done for God can be tainted by sinful attitudes. The only remedy is God's cleansing. For many years, the grain had only given 50 percent of the expected yield and wine had done even worse.

The people re-laid the Temple foundation, and immediately God blessed them. He did not wait for the project to be completed. God often sends his encouragement and approval with our first few obedient steps. He is eager to bless us!

Haggai's final message acknowledged that he was merely the messenger who brings the word of the Lord. It is addressed to Zerubbabel, the governor of Judah. A signet ring was used to guarantee the authority and authenticity of the letter. It served as a signature when pressed in soft wax on a written document. God was reaffirming and guaranteeing his promise of a Messiah through David's line (Matthew 1:12).

God closed his message to Zerubbabel with this huge affirmation: "I have specially chosen you." Such a proclamation applies to us as well; each of us has been chosen by God (Ephesians 1:4). This truth should make us see how much God loves us and motivates us to work for him.

CONCLUSION

Pressures, demands, expectations, and tasks push in from all sides and assault our schedules. Do this! Be there! Finish that! Call them! It seems as though everyone wants something from us—family, friends, employer, school, church, clubs. Soon there is little left to give, as we run out of energy and time. We find ourselves rushing through life, attending to the necessary, the immediate, and the urgent. The important is all too often left in the dust. Our problem is not the volume of demands or lack of scheduling skills, but values—what is truly important to you.

Haggai's message to the people sought to get their priorities straight, help them quit worrying, and motivate them to rebuild the Temple. Like them, we often place a higher priority on our personal comfort than on God's work and true worship. But God is pleased and promises strength and guidance when we give him first place in our life. What has God told you to do? Put all else aside and obey Him. When you feel down, remind yourself: God has chosen me!

www.ingramcontent.com/pod-product-compliance
Lightning Source LLC
Chambersburg PA
CBHW061140230426
43663CB00027B/2986